FINANCIAL

STABILITY

—— FOR LIFE ——

FINANCIAL STABILITY

—— FOR LIFE ——

A Smart, Compassionate Approach to

MAKING THE MOST OF YOUR MONEY

DANIEL E. BUTLER, CFP®

Advantage

Published by Advantage, Charleston, South Carolina.
Member of Advantage Media Group.

ADVANTAGE is a registered trademark, and the Advantage colophon is a trademark of Advantage Media Group, Inc.

Printed in the United States of America.

ISBN: 978-1-59932-695-5
LCCN: 2016934563

This publication is designed to provide accurate and authoritative information in regard to the subject matter covered. It is sold with the understanding that the publisher is not engaged in rendering legal, accounting, or other professional services. If legal advice or other expert assistance is required, the services of a competent professional person should be sought.

Advantage Media Group is proud to be a part of the Tree Neutral® program. Tree Neutral offsets the number of trees consumed in the production and printing of this book by taking proactive steps such as planting trees in direct proportion to the number of trees used to print books. To learn more about Tree Neutral, please visit **www.treeneutral.com.** To learn more about Advantage's commitment to being a responsible steward of the environment, please visit **www.advantagefamily.com/green**

Advantage Media Group is a publisher of business, self-improvement, and professional development books and online learning. We help entrepreneurs, business leaders, and professionals share their Stories, Passion, and Knowledge to help others Learn & Grow. Do you have a manuscript or book idea that you would like us to consider for publishing? Please visit **advantagefamily.com** or call **1.866.775.1696.**

In memory of my father, James E. Butler, who taught me to always see the positive in people and life.

TABLE OF CONTENTS

ACKNOWLEDGMENTS

I would like to express my heartfelt gratitude to my family, clients, friends, and colleagues who saw me through this book from inception to finish. The support provided was certainly much needed and appreciated.

To all those who provided ideas and comments and assisted in the editing and design of the book, I can't thank you enough.

I would also like to thank the people of RJFS for their tremendous support and professionalism over the past twenty-one years. When I first joined RJFS, I was convinced that they were the best financial-services company in the world. After twenty-one years of working with them, those feelings remain unchanged.

Thank you as well to our many wonderful clients, now located in over twenty states throughout the country. Thanks for allowing me to work with you on the development and implementation of your personalized financial plans. More importantly, thanks for your friendship, trust, and confidence.

I would also like to thank my colleagues Jennifer Campbell, Marianne Lucey, and Bob Campbell for their day-to-day support in our quest to provide the world-class service that our clients enjoy and deserve.

And finally, thank you to my wonderful wife Stephanie and our six beautiful children. Your unwavering support of me throughout my career cannot adequately be expressed. The joy, satisfaction, and pride that I receive from being a member of our family are more than anyone could ask for in this lifetime.

INTRODUCTION

THE RETIREE'S WORLD

"Eventually, your clients will look just like you," my older colleague told me one day at lunch. I had recently befriended him at the offices of the Philadelphia brokerage where I had accepted a position not long after graduating from college. He had several decades of experience. I had months.

"What do you mean?" I asked.

"What I mean is that you will soon find out that you will work most effectively with people that think like you, act like you, and generally look at things the way that you do," he said. "It seems the times that I have had the most trouble with people were when we just didn't click."

Nearly thirty years later, I have experienced the wisdom of my old friend's words. The most enduring relationships in my financial-planning practice tend to be with people who have a similar view and outlook on the world as my own. I can work with many types of people, but certain characteristics are essential to a successful relationship.

A central feature of those relationships is trust. The many engineers that come to see me focus their lives primarily on process

1

and detail. Early in our process, they soon tend to trust the accuracy of the information and charts that I provide to them. They appreciate the newfound freedom to move on to other things that they want to pursue in life rather than spending hours at the computer, trying to figure out how their portfolio has performed.

It's unlikely that you will feel that way about every financial advisor you meet. Admittedly, I am not a good fit for everyone. But I am well aware that when I shake hands with people, they sense that I am a man who is trustworthy and competent. You have spent the better part of a lifetime building your nest egg, and now you are looking for a trustworthy professional to relieve you of the burden of managing those assets.

Through the years, people have told me that I am easy to talk to and very transparent throughout the planning process. As new clients and I get to know each other, the conversation and subject matter might, at first, seem a bit random. Initially, there will be two-way dialogue that encompasses one subject; then we might change direction. It may seem arbitrary to some, but I am working to gain a deep understanding of the individual, couple, or family. This is how we initially set out to develop a game plan.

My clients tend to call or e-mail me about a wide variety of issues, some of which are unrelated to their portfolio. On a recent afternoon, a client asked that I join him at his accountant's office to discuss the tax implications of buying a second home. My clients frequently tell me that they want a second opinion on important matters. They seek me out because they have an overall comfort level with the relationship. They have talked to me multiple times, but they see their accountant only once or twice a year. Their estate-planning attorney may only see them once every five years.

Accommodating such requests fills my calendar, but I am happy to help because I know that my clients require my perspective of their overall picture. I recognize specific issues that they and their other professionals may not. I know that being there for my clients is the way to develop loyal and enduring relationships.

I want to ensure that I am consistently in touch with my clients' thinking, wishes, and desires. I want dialogue that encourages them to speak up and push back until they are certain that I know what they want. The value of what I do goes beyond the financial services I provide. More important than crunching the numbers, I help my clients invest their assets in a way that allows them to achieve their goals and live life to the fullest.

THE BEST WAY TO WIN

The biggest fear that I hear from people of retirement age is that they might run out of money. They are looking for reassurance that their assets are sufficient to last the rest of their lives. They want to remain independent. They do not want to become a burden on their children, on their friends, or on society at large.

That is why it is so fundamentally important that I understand what the client is attempting to accomplish in retirement and that I can see the actual amount of resources available to ultimately accomplish that goal. Much of the planning depends upon the desired lifestyle. If attaining an 8 percent annual rate of return is necessary to achieve that lifestyle, you will see quickly from our analysis that the probability of success will be low. If, however, you need only a 3 percent rate of return on your assets to live the way that you want, then success tends to be far more attainable.

In other words, the planning must come first. When the planning is done properly, the portfolio management generally will fall right into place. The planning will help us to see the kind of performance needed to meet your goals and the amount of risk that is tolerable within your portfolio. With clarity, transparency, and an understanding of the details of the plan, you can ensure that you are lowering your probability of running out of money.

Wealth is relative. A couple who has a net worth of approximately $500,000 might not think of themselves as wealthy, but after a thorough analysis, we might discover that a withdrawal rate of only 3.5 percent of their portfolio is necessary after pension and Social Security income. They can be much better off than a couple with several million dollars and a lifestyle that costs $700,000 or $800,000 per year. The size of the asset base often matters less than the percentage of return required to maintain the desired lifestyle and goals. It is purely a matter of expectations. Some people's idea of relaxation is to sit in their backyard garden. Other people's idea of relaxation is to shop in a piazza in Rome.

The five years prior to retirement and the five years afterward can be very tumultuous, financially speaking. The retiree faces multiple changes in life, and the rules have been modified somewhat on the approach to retirement. Many years have been spent accumulating money, and now you will begin using those funds. This is what is known as the *distribution phase* of your financial life.

The key to financial success is to win by not losing. The portfolio's assets must be preserved and positioned to participate in market gains. The assets must also have the ability to generate consistent, tax-efficient income. As you prepare for retirement, care must be taken to avoid excessive risk that could damage your chance of success.

It is important to ask the difficult questions. For example, what would happen if you needed extensive health care over a period of years? These scenarios can be tested, which will serve to either reassure you or to warn you. And the scenarios can be severe: Suppose that a few years before your retirement, a third of your portfolio is lost in a market crash, and then to compound matters, this is followed by a company-wide downsizing, and you lose your job.

Life happens, and you need a plan. In analyzing your needs, we can project your probability of success and assist you in making any necessary adjustments. It may become obvious that you need to postpone one or more of your goals to preserve your lifestyle, home, and future. We can help you to make those critical decisions.

A LONG-TERM RELATIONSHIP

My clients generally range in age from fifty-five to eighty-five years old. I have one client who is one hundred years old. Many of my clients are in the planning stages leading up to retirement. Some are wealthy but don't demand much from their money. They lead a relatively simple lifestyle solely on their pension and Social Security income. Some are physicians, attorneys, corporate executives, or small business owners. They have a wide range of occupations and avocations. They have significant resources but are inconspicuously affluent.

My objective with the majority of clients is rarely to beat the Dow or some other index. Ultimately, it is to help them progress toward a comfortable, confident retirement. I'm not looking for clients who are looking solely for the highest rate of return. Rarely can anyone in our industry beat an index year in and year out. Again, our approach is to progress toward winning by not losing. By definition, this kind of positioning will lead to underperformance when the market is going straight up. But over time, with severe market pullbacks, you may experience less volatility. Our objective for retirees is to achieve 75 percent of the return of an index such as the S&P 500 but with only 50 to 55 percent of the risk. Clients want to know that they will be able to maintain their lifestyle and avoid being a burden on their family and friends.

I enjoy working with clients who want comprehensive financial planning and are willing to provide us with the information necessary to determine their best prospects of a comfortable lifestyle. Sometimes, a prospective client appears reluctant to provide much information at all. In this scenario, it is unlikely that the relationship will continue. Without mutual transparency, the relationship doesn't have staying power.

This is not a book of specific investment advice. This book is for people anticipating retirement who are interested in a long-term relationship with their advisor and in learning about the variety of issues that can ultimately influence their long-term well-being. This is a book for individuals and couples who are thoughtful about the financial direction that their lives will take over the next twenty to forty years and into the next generation.

We begin with the basics: Could you live comfortably right now in retirement, based on your current lifestyle needs and savings? After that, we shift the focus to long-term goals and the decisions necessary to attain those goals. Along the way, you should be working with someone who will be compassionate, direct, and truthful during the entire process.

A CUSTOM DESIGNER

Growing up in the northern suburbs of Chicago, I can recall being intrigued by finances as early as age eleven or twelve. Watching the evening news, I heard about markets, stocks, and the economy. I wondered about a world out there consisting of buyers and sellers, where people placed bets on the future of their ideas and enterprises. Soon, I was picking up books and magazines and reading everything I could about finances. I was certain that one day I would be making my living in the financial-services industry.

When I was a high school senior, my father's employer transferred him to eastern Pennsylvania, where I rejoined my family following graduation. I then enrolled at West Chester University in southeastern Pennsylvania. I particularly recall a professor I had for a macroeconomics class. I would stop by during his office hours regularly to talk about matters that went well beyond the topics of his class. We talked about the markets and how they were interrelated to the economy as a whole. He encouraged me to think independently and outside of the box with regard to economics. He had been very successful in the financial industry and was semiretired. Teaching was something that he was doing for fun, or to give back. I was never able to schedule another class with him, but I would often stop by his office to say hello, and we would chat about the state of the economy.

"This is the only industry I know," he told me, "where people desire to purchase things at full retail price and then sell at a discounted price." It was the first time that I had ever heard that. This was about the time of the 1987 crash. "People who don't have an advisor to talk them through this," he said, "are going to sell right at the bottom."

That was close to three decades ago, and my interactions with that professor were what initially moved me to enter the financial-planning business and eventually help people to manage their money. He stopped teaching at the college the year after my graduation. I learned later that he had passed away, and I regret that we did not stay in touch. But for those two or three impressionable college years, he was a major influence on the course that my career would take.

After college, I worked at a Philadelphia brokerage for several years. My supervisor would print out the daily revenue run and berate any broker whose name wasn't on the first tab. After that, he would walk around making loud and embarrassing comments about the brokers who had less-than-acceptable revenue. It was very disheartening. After a while, having attained a degree of success there, I went out searching for an employer whose philosophies paralleled my own.

I did not want to jump to another firm just for the sake of moving. I wanted to find a progressive, client-friendly corporate culture that gravitated from the top down to both the advisor and the client. I found that culture in Raymond James & Associates, which I joined in 1994. Three years later, in 1997, I was able to move to the independent-contractor division of Raymond James Financial Services, Inc. under a more senior financial planner. This allowed me to be an independent advisor not directly employed by Raymond James. I have been there since because I firmly believe that our firm operates in the best interest of our clients. That, in my opinion, is the best arbiter of success. It is a culture of integrity and professionalism.

In the years since, I have garnered a wealth of knowledge and experience. I founded Butler Financial, an independent-contractor firm under the Raymond James umbrella, in 2004, following a buyout of my more senior financial partner. I maintain a fiduciary responsibility, requiring us to always work in the best interest of our clients.

In essence, I am a manager of risks. The risks that you face in your investment life will be a major element of this book. When you are on the cusp of retirement, these risks can continue for a long time. Some of our clients have been retired for thirty years. It is not unusual for people to live as long in retirement as they did in their working years.

I assist retirees in making decisions on how to appropriately manage their resources. Some of the managed money needs to be relatively safe and accessible, although a portion of the money must grow at a rate that can keep up with inflation.

The financial plans that we design and implement are anything but boilerplate. They are custom designed only after thoroughly getting to know the clients and focusing on their needs, wants, and the specifics of their unique situations. A plan is constructed to provide you with a reasonable opportunity to attain your goals. As time progresses and life happens, we meet to review your plan and to revise it when necessary.

Recently, during a big whipsaw in the market, a client nervously asked me, "What's going to happen to me if this continues to go down?" We pulled up his investments electronically, and I uploaded the current values. Then we ran a series of scenarios. He wanted to see where his game plan would take him in a worst-case scenario. I was able to show him the probabilities and the results.

Your financial plan breathes with you. As you proceed through retirement, your plan will be your guiding document. It sets forth your objectives at the beginning, and you can amend and adjust it to meet your changing situations. It provides a framework for your investments. With your goals and needs clearly in mind, as well as how much risk you will accept, you can avoid overly conservative as well as overly aggressive risk management. It's possible to obtain the proper balance.

AS YOU TURN THESE PAGES

I invite you to come along with me in the chapters ahead to learn what people of retirement age, just like you, have been doing to smooth the way for many prosperous years ahead. We will examine ways in which you can create an income plan designed to last your lifetime.

Along the way, we will talk about the various financial risks that you are likely to face as you move into and through retirement. These include market risk, inflation, taxes, the possible need for long-term care, and other threats. We will discuss how best to manage those risks so that you can preserve your life savings and your estate while also investing your assets to keep up with the cost of living and, ideally, leave an inheritance to your loved ones.

From previous generations, retirement planning has changed dramatically. We will consider the implications of these changes, as pensions have given way to the ubiquitous 401(k), and our Social Security system continues to provide more questions than answers. In this new world, you would do well to seek professional advice. I will assist in guiding you through the many considerations in finding a trustworthy, reliable team that will be with you for many years to come.

CHAPTER ONE

ENTERING NEW TERRITORY

I n 1992, my father was forced into retirement at age sixty-two. He had worked hard for many years to provide for our family. He had earned a good salary, eclipsing $100,000 a year in 1982, when I was seventeen. He had a family of six children to support.

A few years out of college, I was sitting with him one day at a restaurant, and he was reflecting on his career. I shared with him some of the things that I had been learning and showed him a printout that I had made projecting the growth of a portfolio if a mere $100 or $200 a month was consistently invested for thirty years.

"You know," he told me, "back in 1972, I had a friend who got into the financial business, so I put a couple thousand dollars into a fund. I never added anything to it, and when I looked in 1980, it was worth less then when I opened it. So I cashed out. I never really did any investing."

In all of those years, the only investment that my father had ever made was in his home and in the stock of his employer. He had received stock options, purchased stock, and received bonuses in the form of stock. The stock did fairly well, and over time, it amounted to some savings for my mother and him. However, he failed to recognize what I was attempting to illustrate: how a young person, consistently investing just a few hundred dollars a month for decades, could amass an absolutely amazing amount of retirement savings.

This was not information that I had learned at the brokerage where I was working. I had discovered this entirely on my own. I was studying and researching how I might be able to make a living by helping people. I didn't like selling. I hated the feeling that I got when advising someone to buy a hundred shares of this company or that company when I had no clue about that person's specific situation.

Had it not been for my father's pension, he and my mom would have had a tough time of it. They had spent almost everything that he had earned, and even with his significant income, they were living paycheck to paycheck.

Dad died several years after our conversation that day in the restaurant. "I wish I had done things differently," I remember him telling me. "I wish someone had told me these things back then. I wish I'd known someone to step me through it."

The key is to live within your means or just enough below your means so that you can put money away for the long term to let it accumulate. That's the essence of it. My father's pension helped my parents to have a relatively comfortable retirement. But as he ultimately recognized, they could have done much better.

A NEW WORLD OF CONCERNS

Retirement can catch you by surprise. It is a major transition financially, socially, and emotionally, and it can be scary. You are disengaging from your work life and probably will not be seeing as much of the people with whom you worked for years. If much of your identity is tied to your career, you may feel adrift and lost. You may also be spending a lot more time at home with your spouse. Meanwhile, your paychecks will suddenly stop. How will they be replaced?

Frankly, you may find yourself busier than ever, even if you are anticipating leisurely hours of relaxation. I have found that most retirees feel compelled to remain relevant to society. Many take college classes, seek out new experiences, and become involved in a variety of volunteer activities.

Most of the retirees with whom I have dealt over the years have a game plan for the things that they would like to do in retirement. During the first decade or so of retirement, they often are so busy that they cannot easily find the time to meet with me. They are traveling, spending time with their children and grandchildren, and filling their days with a variety of pursuits. They are enjoying a sense of freedom.

Unfortunately, some retirees don't get that experience. They face the prospect of a retirement characterized by worry and struggle. They may have to return to work to make ends meet. Their Social Security benefit and pension, if present, are not enough to cover their bills. For whatever reason, they have not been able to save enough to create a financial cushion. We emphasize the need to set aside three to six months of living expenses to cover any sudden changes or surprises in life. Unfortunately, many people lack the discretionary cash flow to do that. They lack the funds necessary to transition into retirement—especially if it is forced upon them suddenly and prematurely due to a company downsize.

Preparation for retirement needs to be mental, emotional, and financial. My father's retirement at age sixty-two was not optional. His company eliminated his job and wasn't going to reposition him. His job was his identity in so many ways. His friendships were there, and he had not built up social networks outside the workplace. Meanwhile, he was around the house more than usual, and that in itself creates an adjustment that every couple must address. I know that my mother felt that stress. She had her own social life and her own connections.

I regularly address these issues with my clients. One good reason to ensure that you are financially stable is so that you can focus on maintaining emotional and social balance following retirement. This can be a time when loneliness and depression set in. Your retirement planning must account for more than money. It must consider the human need to remain relevant in the world and to maintain healthy connections and relationships.

In retirement, your concerns have changed dramatically from what they were earlier in life, when so many possibilities lay ahead. But that, too, was a time of great stress. Where did you want to live?

Where did you want to raise your children? How would you pay for their education? You found yourself taking on debt for cars or a home or other things that you needed—or *thought* that you needed. Perhaps you spent a lot of money on luxury or discretionary items and focused on keeping up with your peers while neglecting to set enough aside for the retirement that seemed so very far away.

When you are ready to retire, it is likely that you will find your perspective and attitude dramatically changing. Like most people, you will begin to worry about whether you will have enough money to make it through the many years to come. Will you be financially stable for the remainder of your life?

How will you be doing after age seventy-five? This is considered to be the most vulnerable age for retirees. At seventy-five or older, it is highly unlikely that you will be able to go back to work to make up for losses in a portfolio that was paying for your retirement expenses. Additionally, it will be more likely that either you or your spouse will face increased medical costs or the need for long-term care.

You face a world of other concerns. Do you have sufficient liability insurance? Do you have enough money readily available in case of emergency? Do your investments have the ability to keep up with inflation—particularly with the higher rate of inflation that retirees face on certain expenses such as health and medical costs? When you were young, you probably received a regular pay raise that kept pace with inflation. Now, your investments are solely responsible for that raise. You have to build that protection into your retirement income plan. Your investments need sufficient year-to-year gain to keep up with the increased cost of living.

Another major concern is your estate: What will become of it after you pass? Will it go to your heirs? Will you have money left over, and if so, who will receive it? Will it go to charity or your surviving children? If so, do your children want, need, or deserve it? These types of questions often swirl in the minds of prospective retirees. They often have an abiding concern for how their children and grandchildren will progress through life.

In general, this is a time when your financial plan needs to focus increasingly on preserving your assets. You no longer have the many years ahead of you to recover from market dips. If you experience a few bad years right around the time that you are retiring and have left most of your portfolio vulnerable, you may never be able to recover.

IT TAKES TIME

You may have read about how many professional athletes go bankrupt or are under financial stress shortly after they retire—78 percent within two to five years.[1] They made incredible salaries, but how did they invest their money? Where have you invested *your* money? Have you put it into depreciating assets such as cars and furniture, or have you focused on potentially appreciating assets such as your 401(k) with employer match or a savings fund for your children's education?

In the world of sports, athletes that financially succeed—the Magic Johnsons, the Michael Jordans—invest a significant amount of their money in appreciating assets. They focus more on assets that will generate income for them and for their families. Their focus is much less on toys and depreciating assets.

Families of all sizes need to do the same. By systematically putting money into appreciating assets over many years, you will be securing your family's future and protecting yourself from the capri-

---

1 Pablo S. Torre,. "How (and Why) Athletes Go Broke," *Sports Illustrated*, **March 23, 2009.**

cious turns that life can take. And if your company does hand you a severance package and the prospect of retiring early, you can view it as an opportunity rather than as a threat. With all of your planning in place, it can feel more like a jumpstart into retirement rather than a kick out the door.

It takes time to do this right. For young professionals, time is not an issue. With so many investing years ahead, you can take somewhat greater risks, knowing that you will have the time to overcome any losses. This is the accumulation stage of retirement planning. You may feel more inclined to invest aggressively for greater gains. If the market crashes, there is time to wait for the rebound. You are not drawing on your savings to pay for your living expenses. You are in possession of the ultimate commodity: time.

As we all know, that commodity gets to be in increasingly short supply. Yet most retirees still have many years to go. Considering today's typical life expectancy, a couple in their early to midsixties can easily expect to live for twenty or thirty more years. That means financial risk issues must be dealt with as soon as possible. In the three to five years prior to retirement, risk exposure should decrease somewhat, and as you enter into retirement, you can reassess regularly and take an increasingly conservative stance every several years.

At this stage of your life, the portfolio modeling needs to emphasize preservation of capital—taking less risk and tolerating less loss. In the good years, we hope that your gains will outpace your spending needs, although your portfolio likely won't perform as well as one with an aggressive stance. On the flip side, you may be better positioned against a severe loss in a down market. Positives are captured, and negatives are minimized, allowing for a continual progression toward long-term goals. We can establish an estimated annual return that will meet those goals. We aim to outperform that target return when the market will allow it and to preserve your investments when the market experiences a downturn.

When employee compensation stops, there is understandable concern about what will replace that income. The portfolios we design are structured to generate sufficient income for direct deposit into your checking account. Cash flow is paramount to a successful retirement. Unless you face a large spending need, we attempt to avoid removing large pieces from your portfolio to deposit into your checking account. Your income each month should be about the same.

We strive to replicate the pattern to which you are accustomed. There are ways to generate consistent cash flow each month. There are ways to create your own pension if your employer did not provide you with one. There is not as much time on your side as there once was, but there is still sufficient time to achieve what you want to accomplish. It is imperative that the planning be done properly.

ATTAINING TRUE WEALTH

I believe that wealth comes down to the balance between how much you have saved and the costs of the lifestyle that you wish to pursue. Some of the wealthiest people I know do not have much capital on their personal balance sheet. Nonetheless, they have plenty of money for their lifestyle and are very comfortable. True wealth is a matter of deciding what you want to achieve with your capital and ultimately living within your means.

A good financial advisor can help you reach your own definition of wealth that works uniquely for you. Together you can take a close look at your needs versus your wants. What is the cost of shelter, for example? Some people's ideal shelter will cost a lot more than others'.

What some might identify as a want others might consider a need. For example, if your grandchildren live across the country, you may consider it a need to visit them frequently. You don't want to think of that as a negotiable part of your budgeting.

In assessing how to meet your needs and wants, it is necessary to take into consideration all the resources that you have gathered during your lifetime, as well as other income sources such as your pension and Social Security benefit. We look at the various strategies regarding the timing of these benefits and how you might maximize them.

Countless retirees today are concerned about specific issues that weigh heavily on their minds. In my career, I have seen a wide variety of scenarios and themes that often repeat themselves. Individual circumstances, on the other hand, are unique and call for thoughtful planning, advice, and execution. A competent advisor will walk you through the calculations, probabilities, and extensive planning necessary to assist you in getting organized.

CHAPTER TWO

WHAT'S IT ALL ABOUT?

A gentleman that came to see me in 1999 needed to confide in me about something serious. We chatted for a while, and then he looked into my eyes, lowering his voice: "Dan, it's not looking good for me. I have a rare condition,"—he told me the long medical name for it—"and I might only have a year or two to live."

He explained that he and his wife would be traveling to the Northeast, where he would participate in a medical trial for an experimental procedure. "That might buy me some more time, maybe a decade or so, but who knows? Who really knows?"

I witnessed the breadth of his struggle, and it went beyond worrying about dying. He was worried about his spouse, whom he had purposely not asked to join our meeting. He wanted to talk with me frankly about arranging for her to live comfortably after he passed away, whenever that might be. He needed to talk about two scenarios: one in which he would pass soon and another in which he might live for years.

The couple spent several weeks with the clinicians at the hospital, and the ensuing two years brought further procedures. During that time, his prognosis improved markedly. He lived many more years, in which he got to see his children marry and grandchildren born. He passed away at age seventy-five.

On the day when he first came to see me, we began to design two plans: one in which he would be gone, and his wife would carry on without him, financially secure, and another in which he would be very much alive, whether it be for five years or ten or the fifteen with which he was blessed. We talked about what their needs and wants in life would be if they could continue to spend those years together. We considered the possibilities and worked through the details. We talked about the timing of his pension and of the Social Security options available to them. They had not yet reached retirement age, so we needed to work through some of the "what-if" projections.

Once we had those two scenarios designed, it was a matter of waiting to see which we would institute. As his prognosis improved, we increasingly looked at the additional stresses on their finances that resulted from both of them living and enjoying a longer life together. They enjoyed certain activities separately and others that they did together. It seemed that they would spend a long retirement together, until his condition returned and ultimately took him.

This medical crisis had been a wake-up call. It gave that couple an opportunity to think deeply about what really mattered to them and time to reflect on their goals. Later, in gratitude, my client transferred shares of his company to the medical center that treated him. It served as a thank-you for many more years of life—life lived to the fullest.

DEFINING PRIORITIES

We are all on a search for significance. It is an instinct that might lie dormant for years, but later in life, most people find themselves reflecting upon and wondering about the many mysteries of life. They begin contemplating the most important things in life. They think about ties to their family and community. It is absolutely paramount that your financial advisor understands this fundamental human characteristic.

What is it that you want to achieve during your lifetime? Now is the time that you get to the heart of such matters. When your life is nearing its end, what will have made you fulfilled? To have seen your children become independent and successful? To have traveled extensively and experienced cultures across the world? To have left a philanthropic legacy to the institutions and charities that you value?

For many people, family matters most. The goals and aspirations of many retirees center on being part of the lives of their children and grandchildren. They want to be part of the cycle of life, and that is how they continue to remain relevant. I consistently have open discussions regarding these matters with my clients. What is their unique definition of *relevance*?

Their answers have everything to do with their financial-planning decisions. Clients often tell me how important it is to them that their loved ones have fond memories of them. That leads to my next question: How do you make those memories? Will they be made by playing croquet together in the backyard or by traveling to another continent several times a year? Once the objective is known, we can determine the costs of achieving it. If it is possible, we try to find a solution, although it could mean postponing retirement or reprioritizing investments.

We also discuss my role in helping them to attain their definition of *relevance*. I assist in easing their worries about outliving their money so that they can progress through life confidently and focus on their priorities. Toward that end, we focus initially on defining those priorities. We can then proceed with the specifics and details of accomplishing them.

THE RISK OF NOT KNOWING

Many people think of financial planning as being solely about investments. It encompasses much more. It includes granular details of investing, spending, and money management. But broader topics of estate planning, tax planning, and risk assessment are also included. We will be looking more closely at these matters in the chapters ahead, but sound financial planning must start with the big picture. Where are you going? Unless your financial plan addresses that question, it will be more of a generic commentary than a focused strategy.

Much of the financial-planning industry only skims the surface of comprehensive financial planning. Sometimes it seems as if planners only conduct such questioning because their firms require it prior to moving forward with the actual investments. In my view, the overall plan is the exciting part, and it is an essential part. When the plan is designed correctly, progressing to the investment particulars comes naturally. Knowing how much investment risk is needed to accomplish the goals that you have set forth makes it easier to progress.

I believe that the only way to effectively begin a working relationship is to first gain a complete understanding of what the client wants out of life. A surprisingly large number of people simply have not slowed down long enough to ponder the matter. If they have an idea of what they would like to accomplish, it might be out of line with the resources at their disposal. The risk of not knowing is a significant problem that gets in the way of retirement success.

One couple might set out into retirement determined to pursue the dreams that have been put off for years. There are countless items on their bucket lists that they still want to pursue. They envision elaborate trips, a new home, and much more. Unfortunately, they have long been out of the habit of living within their means. Having indulged themselves for years, they are now at a time of reckoning. They simply do not have the income to finance their wants.

Another couple might be in relatively good shape financially and not even know it. Instead, they are living in fear, afraid of losing everything that they have managed to gain. And so they sit tight. They do not avail themselves of the many opportunities now available to them. They miss out on so much because they are unaware of what they are now able to do. This might be a severe example, but to some extent, it describes many people. They are incapable of seeing everything that their savings are now able to provide. From their perspective, those savings seem sadly insufficient.

I help people become aware of their options. Many of our clientele live below their means to some extent. That is how they were able to save so much. Generally, there is much we can do to usher them into a productive retirement. Where it becomes more challenging is in dealing with people who have been living at their means or slightly above their means. It seems that many people tend to overspend when they are young, but as those pay raises come in, they eventually start putting more money aside.

Of the two couples described, it is the latter scenario that I see most often. These couples have attained significant wealth but are living conservatively. Occasionally, this can reach an extreme. Frugality within reason and when warranted is admirable. When it is excessive, it comes across as cheap and sometimes irritating. Sometimes, extreme behavior results from fear of the unknown. Some older retirees recall the struggles of the Great Depression during their childhood. Those memories linger and distort their present-day reality. We can help to bring the truth out of the shadows.

When you better understand your financial positioning and can see clearly the options available, you will gain confidence. That is what I do for my clients. I illustrate to them how to make the best use of their money so that they can live a comfortable and fulfilling lifestyle. Such a lifestyle does not require an enormous amount of wealth. Many people of moderate means—less than $1 million of liquid net worth—can actually be among the most balanced in what they can do for themselves, their children, and their grandchildren.

A TIME FOR EVERY PURPOSE

These are the kind of questions to be asking yourself:

1. What is important to you?

2. What makes you happy and fulfilled?

3. How will you be remembered?

4. Where would you like to go, whom would you like to help, and what would you still like to learn?

5. Is there anything that you have wished you had time to do?

6. What would you say is your principal purpose in life?

Try writing down your dreams and goals. You will have made a significant step toward designing the game plan of your life. Once words are dedicated to paper, they take on a new priority. The objectives become tangible. They can be organized, prioritized, and pursued.

Think about a time line for these accomplishments. When you consider these goals and how much they will cost, when will you be spending that money? In your sixties? In your nineties? In my many years of working with older people, I have noticed the typical spending pattern of retirees. It is a pattern so prevalent that it needs to be incorporated into the overall financial plan.

In the first ten to twelve years of retirement, couples often spend freely. If they have planned well, enough financial resources are available to them to do pretty much whatever they want. Their cost of living is not much different from what it was before they retired. That begins to change by their midseventies. Their cost of living begins to decline, and overall spending slows. That could be due to health issues, as it becomes more difficult to get around, or it might be by choice: "We've done a lot; we don't need to go to Europe again."

Such is the typical course of the pursuit of one's goals and dreams. Sometimes, planners will recite the common wisdom that living expenses in retirement are 80 percent of what they were previously. Based on our experience, we find that to be inaccurate. We have found that expenses generally do not decline until retirees are well into their seventies, and then the expenses drift downward until the time when one or both spouses require long-term care.

Your individual situation, of course, will determine the design of the financial plan. It must not be based on assumptions that are inaccurate and unrealistic for you. In our regular meetings, I ask clients about their cash flow. Is it enough? Are you feeling constrained? We seek to define your objectives, determine whether you are in line with your resources, and project the timing of those expenses to make sure that the money will be there when you need it. Are you overreaching? Or might you be capable of accomplishing more than you imagined?

Prospective retirees sometimes have a distorted idea about how much of a return they can expect from their market investments. They might estimate that if they have saved $1 million, the market will give them 10 percent, or $100,000, annually. If I hear a couple say something like that, I know that it is time for a reality check.

Part of what we discuss is the concept of "sequence of returns." Markets rise, and markets fall.

None of us can control how the economy behaves, and if that couple needs to withdraw their 10 percent, regardless, for living expenses, they are putting their portfolio at risk. If the down years come early in retirement, and they continue to withdraw that money, their portfolio will quickly erode. Their million-dollar beginning balance could become $800,000 after the first year, and within a

WHAT'S IT ALL ABOUT?

few years could be worth only 50 percent of its original value. It is unlikely that the couple could ever recover the original wealth on which they had pinned their dreams.

That is why it is a good idea to pay off your mortgage, either prior to retiring or shortly thereafter. Eliminating the mortgage payment can provide you with a great deal of flexibility. In the absence of a sizable fixed expense, you are better able to endure sequence-of-return risk. Some might point to the fact that a mortgage provides a tax deduction on the interest. While this is true, an accountant might help you weigh the relative advantage of that savings. Think about how much more can be gained when you are not forced to withdraw that mortgage payment from your portfolio, month after month, during years when the market is tumbling.

GETTING ORGANIZED

In order to organize life's goals and priorities, you need to make sure that your paperwork is in good order. The documents that define your financial life must not be scattered around the house. They need to be filed and stored securely and conveniently for easy reference.

If you decide to work with us, we will ask that you bring in a variety of those documents. It is necessary to review your assets, liabilities, income, investments, and any insurance that you may have. It might feel daunting to gather all of these materials, but we need to evaluate your specific situation. For example, you should provide the following:

- the declaration pages of your homeowners, automobile, umbrella, and life insurance policies and your long-term care coverage

- information on all of your real estate, including cost-basis information

- recent statements or online printouts from your accounts that list assets and their current value, cost basis, and titling specifics

- full information on IRAs or 401(k)s, including beneficiary designations

- estate-planning documents such as wills, trusts, and powers of attorney

- documents showing how real property is titled within a trust

- mortgage and loan documents, including credit-card and auto-loan statements

Spending analysis is also an important process. We provide budget worksheets to assist you with itemizing regularly occurring expenditures. As you write them down, you will begin to see specifically where the money goes. Some expenses are less obvious than others. We try to produce a budget that reasonably reflects your spending patterns. We take an inventory of your assets and compare it to your list of needs and wants. Have you been replacing your car every five years? Is that a necessity or a desire?

We will make copies of your documents and return your originals. At home, you should maintain a filing system in a safe that includes your policies and documents. We can help you develop a system, addressing procedures that should be followed in the event of an emergency. These procedures give children or relatives a starting point should an emergency occur; in your safe, they would locate specific directions on the front page of your information binder,

WHAT'S IT ALL ABOUT?

instructing them to see your financial advisor for further information on the documentation contained within the binder. It would also list other team members, including the name of the attorney who drew up the will or trust, and it would clearly list beneficiary designations for accounts and insurance policies.

OPEN COMMUNICATION

It is up to you how much of your financial life to share with your loved ones. Some people are quite open with their children regarding these matters, while others share almost nothing. The dynamics of every family are different, but in general, it can help to provide for a smooth transition when information is readily available and the lines of communication are open. We have found that this becomes more important as the parents grow older and become less able to handle their own financial affairs.

In one case, the parents were in their late eighties, living in a house with a leaking roof and driving a dilapidated car. They kept the heat at sixty degrees in the winter and lived like paupers. While they rarely discussed the specifics of their situation with their son and his wife, a meeting with all four of them together prompted a discussion. After the others had left, the son paused at my office door. "I can't believe this. I just can't believe this! My parents have well over a million dollars on hand—and they're sitting there in that moldy house? They kept telling us they had nothing, no money at all!"

This scenario happens frequently. Communication breaks down, or it was never really established. Sometimes, families find it uncomfortable or believe it is inappropriate to discuss financial matters. The topic can be intimidating. People might shy away from money issues that they have found to be contentious. Estate planning, in particu-

31

lar, involves contemplating the prospect of dying. It can be easier to just not think about it.

You face significant risk when procrastinating on important financial matters and decisions. Outdated beneficiaries on an IRA account or insurance policy are just one example. The inability to make a decision is, in itself, a decision. Doing nothing will have a major impact upon your legacy. For example, if you were to suddenly pass away much earlier than anticipated and had not done any planning, you would be leaving a lot of work for your survivors. Some might call that inconsiderate. As they try to sort it all out, family members may become frustrated and argue among themselves.

This can be prevented by taking timely action to get your affairs in good order. Being proactive with these matters demonstrates to your loved ones that you cared enough to properly plan. This planning should not be delayed until your eighties or nineties, either. People of advanced age sometimes begin to think with less clarity. These matters should be handled promptly and diligently during a time when you are mentally sharp.

The principles are the same at any age: if you can envision your goals, you can work backward to put a plan in place for accomplishing them. When you know where you are going, you can choose the appropriate investments that will provide you with the smoothest ride to the destination.

So much of a successful journey depends on a detailed map. You need to attend to matters both large and small and to sharpen your organizational skills. This is a time to clarify your goals, establish your priorities, and put together the paperwork of your financial life. As you approach retirement, time is of the essence. You must get started sooner rather than later.

CHAPTER
THREE

YOU'RE IN
CHARGE NOW

When my father retired, his pension amounted to about $65,000 a year. For a retiree withdrawing 4 percent each year, that would amount to a nest egg of about $1.6 million. On top of that, he and my mother had a combined Social Security benefit of about $30,000 a year. Together, that pension and benefit played a critical role in providing them with a comfortable retirement.

Unfortunately, they still had a $200,000 mortgage on their home, which was costing them $1,300 a month, not counting taxes and insurance. Without his pension, I do not know how my parents would have survived financially. The pension played the central role in their retirement. They had a few hundred thousand dollars in savings—not enough to significantly boost their retirement income—and their Social Security benefit would have been insufficient to allow them to keep their home. Without the pension, their lifestyle would have been severely compromised.

Many of today's retirees, and those nearing that milestone, still have some kind of pension. Some of those pensions, however, have been frozen at some point and are no longer accumulating. Many other people have no pension at all; employers have long since replaced them with the 401(k) or similar retirement plans. A 2008 survey found that the number of employees covered by pension plans had fallen over twenty-five years from 38 percent to 20 percent nationwide. The credit crisis has caused that number to fall even more since 2008.[2]

The defined benefit has become the defined contribution. In other words, it has become primarily employees' responsibility to save for retirement—not employers' responsibility to take care of them. For employees who have not adjusted to that change in mind-set, the situation is challenging. If you start early, it can be a daunting task to save sufficiently for retirement. If you do not begin investing until you are nearing fifty, it becomes exponentially more difficult. It is essential to start early and invest regularly, whether through a 401(k) plan or some other means.

2 Barbara A. Butrica, Howard M. Iams, Karen E. Smith, and Eric J. Toder, "The Disappearing Defined Benefit Pension and Its Potential Impact on the Retirement Incomes of Baby Boomers," *Social Security Bulletin*, 69, no. 3 (2009), https://www.ssa.gov/policy/docs/ssb/v69n3/v69n3p1.html.

A financial advisor can put you on the right path. Traditionally, advisors talked about "the three-legged stool" of retirement planning. One leg was the pension, the second was Social Security, and the third was whatever savings and investments you had managed to build up over the years. My parents were lucky that they had strength in two of those legs, even though their savings leg was weak. Countless people are looking to retire but don't have a strong stool. They have no pension plan, Social Security solvency concerns them, and their nest egg is modest.

They are justifiably concerned. The Social Security Administration projects that it will only have enough money, under its current structure, to maintain benefits until 2033. After that, the system would only be collecting enough from payroll taxes to pay 75 percent of the current benefits. Retirees face the very real possibility that their benefits may one day be curtailed unless the government takes additional action. It may not be a significant threat to current retirees, but people in their forties and early fifties must account for that possibility when projecting their retirement income.

Social Security has been stretched far beyond its original intent. In the 1930s, when the system was inaugurated, life expectancy was much shorter, and for every retiree who received a benefit, many workers were contributing payroll taxes to the system. In 1955, every retiree was backed by more than eight workers. Today, that number has reduced to three workers, and that is expected to decrease to two by 2030.[3] Our population has seen a huge increase in the number of centenarians among us. Some people have been drawing benefits for nearly as many years as they were employed.

It is clear what is happening. The baby boomers are becoming the retiree boomers, and they are living far longer than just a few

---

3 Ibid.

years into retirement. A typical married couple retiring today is expected to draw about $600,000 from the Social Security system during their lifetimes, according to an Urban Institute study.[4]

A thirty-year-old who today earns $49,000 would receive $1,945 per month upon retirement, as measured in 2015 dollars. However, by the time he or she turns sixty-seven in 2052, the monthly benefit under current rules would be $7,475 per month, according to Social Security Administration estimates.[5] Over the next twenty-five years, the total of that monthly benefit would be nearly $2.2 million.

How can the Social Security system support those kinds of benefits without major changes? The evidence points to the need for younger couples to focus on saving as much as possible for the future, to obtain professional guidance, and to figure Social Security and Medicare benefits into the equation only when they are near retirement. They can control how much they save. They can't control the politics of entitlement programs.

In working with our clients, we project retirement income based on a number of scenarios. For example, we will run a scenario in which the Social Security benefit stays the same. We will run another scenario in which the Social Security benefit is reduced by 50 percent, in the event of means testing or some other major change to the system. And we will run a third scenario in which you never receive a benefit. Then we compare all those projections. Obviously, with a smaller or nonexistent Social Security benefit, you are less likely

4 Barbara A. Butrica, Howard M. Iams, and Karen E. Smith, "The Disappearing Defined Benefit Pension and Its Potential Impact on the Retirement Incomes of Baby Boomers," *Social Security Bulletin*, 65, no. 3 (2003/3004), https://www.ssa.gov/policy/docs/ssb/v65n3/v65n3p1.html.
5 Social Security Administration,. https://www.ssa.gov/planners/retire/AnypiaApplet.html.

to attain your savings goals. You need to examine and review the entire picture with your advisor. Have a thorough understanding of what will happen to your lifestyle if an uncontrollable force eliminates or greatly reduces your benefit. Ideally, your own savings can be enhanced to the point that you don't need to be concerned with Social Security.

Medicare benefits are already subjected to means testing. How much you receive depends on how much support you need. Your Medicare premium is currently based on your adjusted gross income. The concern is that somewhere down the road, to shore up Social Security, the government will start looking at your tax return and subject that benefit to means testing as well. After all, the government already has the data about you to determine your Medicare premium. It would be a simple step to link the existing Medicare data to your Social Security.

When it comes to making sure that your portfolio can meet the challenge, we look at everything extremely conservatively. We imagine life without Social Security. This way, you are aware of what could happen if you have to survive solely on your own savings. We examine all the various scenarios, and we update them as conditions change. When you review your situation and choices repeatedly with a trusted financial advisor, you will have a much higher probability of success. When the government does begin to make changes that could reduce your benefit, it won't come as a shock to you. You will feel prepared.

WHEN SHOULD YOU RETIRE?

A common question among soon-to-be retirees is whether they should begin taking the Social Security benefit early at age sixty-two, at the full retirement age of sixty-six, or at age seventy. One of the first questions that I usually ask concerns your family's longevity history. I'll ask a husband and wife how long each of their parents lived. How long did their grandparents live? My own grandparents lived into their early eighties, and my parents lived into their early nineties. With improvements in health care, there is a higher probability of living a long life.

If longevity runs in your family, then we may decide to postpone your benefits so that the monthly payment will grow larger as time progresses. Much depends upon whether you have enough assets to sustain yourself without Social Security. Among my clients today, I have couples who are deferring their Social Security benefit. They have calculated that they will be better off by spending down their assets at a somewhat higher percentage for several years while the amount of their future benefit grows annually, reaching its peak at age seventy.

The decision to delay until age seventy can result in a far greater combined Social Security benefit over the course of a couple's retirement. However, the decision to take that route needs to be preceded by a frank discussion: if the people in your family do not typically live long lives, and particularly if either or both of you are in failing health, then it may not make sense to delay receiving the income. If you elect to delay collecting the full benefit until age seventy rather than claiming it at age sixty-six, you will be forgoing four years of payments in exchange for a larger benefit. However, the break-even point doesn't occur until your late seventies to early eighties, depending upon your date of birth. If your parents have died in their sixties or seventies, you may decide that the odds of living longer are against you and choose to begin benefits earlier.

Many other variables can enter into the equation on which benefit option makes sense for you. To learn more, a Certified Financial

Planner™ (CFP®) is an excellent place to start. You can also check with the Social Security Administration (ssa.gov), but you will need to research their resources thoroughly to determine the best strategy for you. I can provide sophisticated comparisons for clients in my office.

Many personal and household factors can influence Social Security benefits. The most significant factor is the age at which you opt to begin benefits. Below is a range of benefits that would be received depending on what age at which you opt to receive them. This does not include the impact of spousal benefits (if married), which can make a significant difference.

The following graphs illustrate the importance of knowing when to begin collecting Social Security benefits.

PRIMARY WAGE EARNER

Note: Estimated Benefits If Paid in Maximum during Working Years

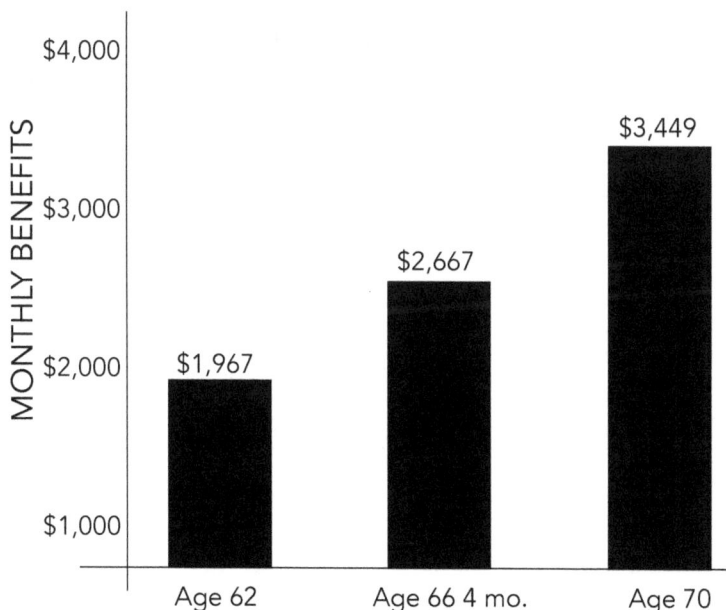

This is a hypothetical illustration.

SPOUSE

Note: Limited Contributions to Social Security during Working Years

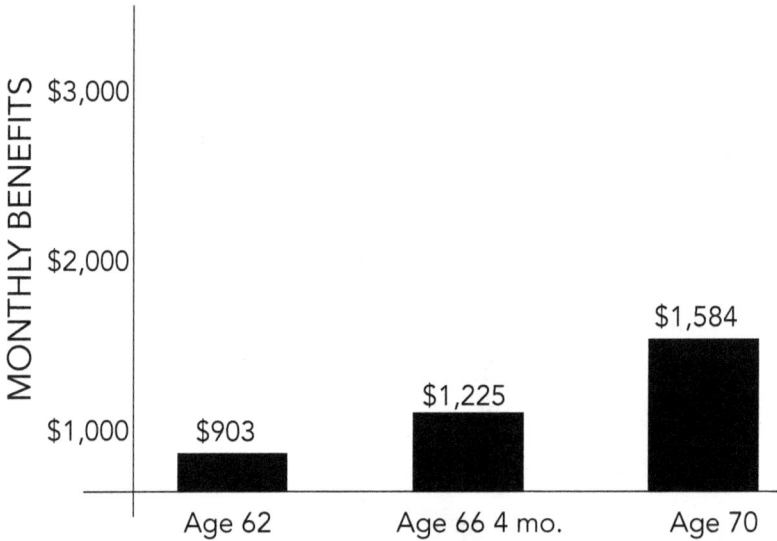

This is a hypothetical illustration.

Family history, as mentioned previously, also plays a significant role in when you opt to receive benefits. Please see the graph below.

Family History	Estimated Cumulative Benefits		
	Age 62	**Age 66 & 4 Months**	**Age 70**
Life Expectancy = 80	$633,164	$604,032	$655,974
Life Expectancy = 90	$986,600	$1,208,064	$1,136,034
Life Expectancy = 100	$1,340,036	$1,812,096	$1,616,094

The below graph further illustrates the importance of claiming strategies and the break-even points for various age groups.

MONTHLY BENEFIT AMOUNTS DIFFER BASED ON THE AGE YOU DECIDE TO START RECEIVING BENEFITS

This example assumes a benefit of $1,000 at full retirement age of 66

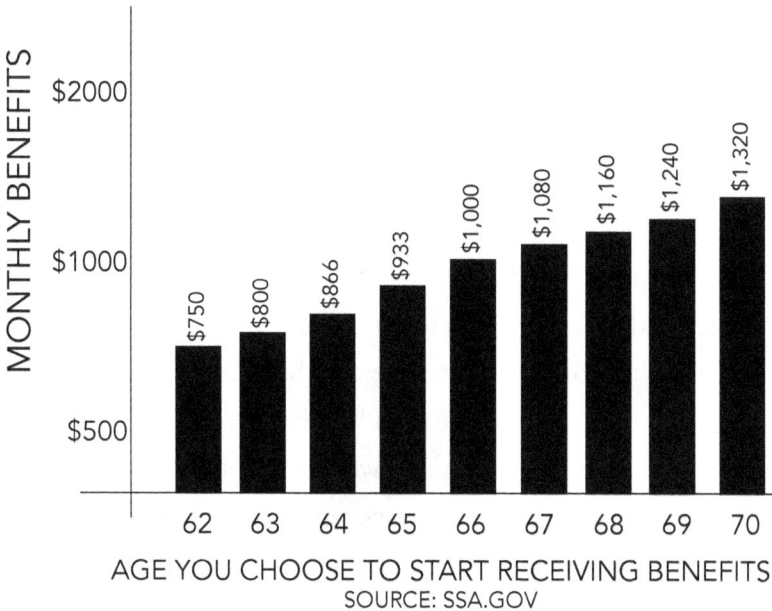

AGE YOU CHOOSE TO START RECEIVING BENEFITS

SOURCE: SSA.GOV

This is a hypothetical illustration.

THE RISE OF THE 401(K)S

Pensions (defined-benefit plans), once the bedrock of retirement planning, today have largely been replaced by defined-contribution plans, such as 401(k)s, 403(b)s, IRAs, and similar plans. This change came about in large part because pensions were becoming highly costly to businesses. They had been popular from the 1950s through the 1980s; employers saw them as a way to tie their workers to the company. A pension was an incentive for employees to stay put for many years, and the prevailing management style of the time saw workforce stability as a key driver of success.

Those were also decades in which the United States was one of the largest growth economies in the world. World War II had destroyed many economies, and they needed to be rebuilt. The United States had that postwar capability. As we got into the 1980s, however, we saw globalization of economic growth, as companies from a variety of nations pushed for global market share.

US companies found themselves taking care of an army of retired employees. The pension plans were an enormous expense, and the companies bore all the responsibility of a severe market downturn. During economic slumps, when corporate earnings declined, the companies had to increase their contributions to the defined-benefit plans at the worst possible time for them. Meanwhile, foreign companies that did not provide such benefits were able to offer their products and services at a much lower cost. The old-style pension plan began to be seen as an expensive endeavor that hurt the competitive edge of large US corporations.

With the advent of 401(k) plans in the late 1970s and early 1980s, the onus of retirement savings switched largely to the employees. They could set aside a portion of their salary, sometimes matched by the employer, into an investment account that would allow growth to accrue, tax-deferred, until retirement. The employer might offer some amount of profit sharing at its discretion.

Companies soon realized that the arrangement gave them tremendous flexibility. They could reduce or eliminate their profit-sharing contributions during a recession. And once the employee left the company, there was no legacy cost. In other words, the company didn't have to pay a lifelong pension to former employees, some of whom might have left a decade or two previously. In a globally competitive world, the expense of defined-benefit pension plans became just too much.

That trend continued through the eighties and into the nineties, as many companies shut down their pension plans. In doing so, they were freed from the lifelong obligation to former employees, and they no longer had to shore up those plans during down years. Some employees saw the 401(k)s as giving them a new freedom to advance in their careers and move without financial penalty to a new company. No longer did they feel attached by an umbilical cord to the company that would be feeding them their pension one day.

In today's world, the 401(k) is portable. As you change employers, you can transfer the account to a new custodian and consolidate it with the 401(k) of your new employer. You can roll the money over easily and without penalty, if you do so directly. The tax deferral continues. In fact, it is important that you do consolidate your accounts: you do not want to have several 401(k)s floating around, because inevitably you will not manage them as well. By rolling them into a single account, you will maintain better control. And in these changing times, when you and not the company have become increasingly responsible for managing your financial well-being during retirement, you want to have as much control as possible.

CHAPTER FOUR

A FOUNDATION OF TRUST

"We have been saving 7 percent of our salaries," the woman visiting my office proclaimed, "and what we want to know is whether we can retire." She motioned to her husband, who sat quietly. They had made it clear that she was the primary breadwinner and that he was not much involved in the family's financial affairs. One of my clients had referred them to me.

The woman then pulled out a tablet upon which she had written several pages of questions. They were good questions, actually, and the type you might find on a list of "good questions to ask a potential financial advisor." It was clear that she wanted answers but also that she did not want to provide the information necessary to answer her questions specifically.

"Well," I said, "there is a lot more that I would need to know before I can give you any kind of answer that would make sense. Yes, 7 percent is a good savings rate. But I don't know anything about the kind of lifestyle that you want to lead or how much money you would need to do that. I don't know how much you already have saved or even what your salaries are. I don't know how long people in your family tend to live."

"So do you have enough to retire? Here's my answer: I don't know." She hadn't provided me with a fraction of the information that would be needed before I could tell them anything. I asked whether she had brought any financial statements or estate-planning documents with her so that I could jot down some notes and try to get her some answers.

"No, I'd like the answers now," she said. "I'm not going to divulge any of my personal information to you at this juncture. I just want some answers."

I responded, "I'm reluctant to answer most of these questions until I know enough about you and your husband's situation to provide you with advice that would be of any value." I explained to her that if she went to a doctor but refused to answer any questions or talk about her symptoms, she couldn't expect much help. The doctor wouldn't have a clue whether she had a headache, stomachache, or the flu.

A trusting relationship requires give and take. My clients are generally quite open to discussion and review of their financial situation, even during our initial meeting. This couple left after an hour and didn't return, which was expected. It was obvious that they were not a good fit.

GETTING TO THE HEART OF THE MATTER

During the first meeting, I generally can get a good read on whether a productive relationship can be developed. Usually within thirty minutes, I can sense the level of trust that is likely to develop. Over the years, I have come to recognize what motivates people, what holds them back, and why they present themselves the way they do.

I recently met with a prospective client who had just been terminated from his job. He had attained a reasonable amount of wealth in his career and was actively seeking new employment. One of his first comments to me was, "We can talk about this, but I'm not sure I'm going to do anything."

"And that's all right," I told him, "because I'm not asking you to do anything." But I had to wonder why he would say that. As we talked, he came across to me as stern and very much used to being in control. I wondered whether he felt that he had lost that control and his demeanor was masking that fear. At times he sounded evasive, but it didn't seem to emanate from an untrusting nature. Rather, he seemed to be looking for some measure of reassurance of his value. Losing a job can shake your foundation and your sense of identity. Perhaps he felt as if he would be relinquishing control of his finances, too. His worry proved unfounded. His track record demonstrated that he had been doing a good job, both in his career and in managing his portfolio.

I try to understand what people bring to the table. It's more than the data that I need to interpret. I need to get a feel for the emotions and motivations that drive their financial concerns and decisions. It is paramount that I know what they have gone through and what they are currently going through. Once it is clear that we can trust each other, people tend to let down their defenses, and communication becomes much easier and more effective.

I can certainly understand those defenses. They are normal and human. What gets in the way is a wall of distrust or an air of secrecy. If I see an obstacle to a long-term relationship, I let the prospective client know how I perceive the situation as soon as possible. Not everyone who comes in to see me is honest with the process. Some do not share essential information. In those cases, it would be better to shake hands and part ways at the outset. If there is no commitment, it just won't work.

Family dynamics can play a large role in the overall planning process. For example, a couple has recently become grandparents and wants to open a college fund. Can they do so without jeopardizing their own retirement? If we have built a relationship over time, the couple will trust my advice. The challenge is to reach the level where my clients will confide in me that they have, say, a thirty-year-old child who seems unmotivated or a spendthrift child who perpetually seems to be in need.

Sharing such details comes naturally as we forge a long-term relationship. In fact, because that relationship is so important, we don't charge for the up-front planning. People are welcome to take the plan and attempt to institute it themselves. But I know from experience that life happens, the plan is forgotten, and they will be off track a few years later. By contrast, my staff and I follow up regularly with careful reviews, reminders, and updates. It cannot be emphasized enough: the relationship is constantly evolving and ongoing.

A professional planner takes the time to understand your expectations. That is why I ask questions that I know you won't hear from other planners: How often do you replace your car? How often do you travel, and how much do you spend? Do you help out your children, and what are their expenses? Even if they are out on their own, have you still been helping them? Often I find that a lot of money goes to children or grandchildren to pay for college or other expenses. We must account for that in the budgeting, or the client could experience a severe shortfall later in retirement.

Seeing the big picture leads to the best recommendations. I cannot effectively help unless I fully understand your expectations. We start by establishing the basic level of what it costs to keep a roof over your head. If we can't get to that point, it is unlikely that we will be working together. Trust is the core of any solid relationship, whether between client and advisor or husband and wife.

Typically, our clients are married couples, and we recognize and respect the importance of involving both spouses in the discussions. They tend to have different views, and it is important that we understand both. A lot of times, one spouse is more conservative and reluctant to participate fully in the discussion until the second or third meeting. In these cases, I will turn to that spouse to draw him or her in with questions like, "So how do you feel about the cost of living? Is it in line? How do you feel about the children? How much help do they need?" Generally, both spouses will then open up, and that helps all of us reach a deeper level of understanding.

IN YOUR BEST INTEREST

When people come to see me, they often need help with a major life event. But underlying the crisis of the moment is their need for a custom-designed financial plan. Perhaps they have worked with another advisor and are looking for a different perspective. If I determine that the other advisor has been doing a good job, I will acknowledge that, even if it means losing an opportunity. If a relationship has already been formed, they should probably think twice before abandoning it.

However, sometimes I hear that they are dissatisfied with their previous advisor because he or she seemed distant. Most of my new clients previously have had accounts with many different financial firms and want more personalized service. I make it a point to listen intently and ensure that I understand their goals in life, their current wishes, their future goals, and their desires following their demise. With that in mind, I work with their other advisors, such as their CPA and estate attorney, to coordinate the specialized planning.

I am a fiduciary. I am required to suggest only strategies that will be in my clients' best interest. I have discovered that I can make a good living by doing the right thing, which means doing only what is best for my clients and not for anyone else. For example, annuities can be appropriate in certain circumstances, but when clients ask about purchasing one, I make sure that they understand the pluses and minuses. I explain that the person selling the annuity is getting a commission up front of 5 or 6 percent. "Does that salesperson fully understand your financial situation?" I ask. Sometimes I do include an annuity in my own clients' financial plans, but I fully disclose any fees and commissions and carefully explain the specific purpose within the portfolio.

Doing the right thing means designing a plan appropriate for your specific stage of life, whether you are in your forties and just starting to imagine retiring someday or you have been retired for two or three decades. In serving my clients in the late stages of retirement, I have often worked with the people to whom they have given powers of attorney. I discuss with them the nature of my relationship with the client and my understanding of his or her wishes. And many times, those same people become clients of mine. They tell me that they appreciate my emphasis on a lifelong relationship, which is something they lacked with their previous advisor.

How can you know who will be best for you? What should you be looking for in a financial advisor, and what do all those letters after the name mean, anyway? Preferably, look for an advisor who is a CFP® in good standing with the Certified Financial Planning Board of Standards, Inc. It means that you will be working with someone who has agreed to serve as a fiduciary and do only what is in the client's best interest. That person has had extensive training, testing, and continuing education to remain in good standing. You can go to the CFP® website and find a CFP® in your area, or you can ask your friends for referrals to such professionals.

It is unlikely that you will have a fiduciary relationship with a stockbroker. There are plenty of good stockbrokers whose advice may fit your needs, but understand that their standard is to provide you with investments that are suitable but not necessarily in your best interest. The stockbroker's primary allegiance could very well be to the company for which he or she is employed.

For the long term, you should know that your best interests are at the heart of every discussion. It's as if you have entered into a marriage of sorts, based on a deep understanding of each other. We work together to reach a common goal: your long-term financial success.

ONE SIZE CAN'T FIT ALL

It is unlikely that you will have that sort of relationship with your neighborhood friends or office colleagues. For starters, they may be at an entirely different stage of life than you. What they might find financially appropriate might prove disastrous in your own portfolio. A great investment for a thirty-year-old could prove to be a terrible choice for a sixty-year-old.

Nor should you pay too much attention to the "advice" that you hear on the television or radio. The pundits of the airwaves and cable channels know nothing about your financial situation and therefore cannot sensibly prescribe particular products that will serve you best. Occasionally, I receive calls from nervous clients who have been watching various business news channels. I politely remind them that the media, in their quest for an audience, lean toward the sensational. It's as true for financial news as it is for any other coverage. Sure, you can get tidbits of good information, but you can also get ulcers from hearing talking heads predicting a market sell-off or a plunge in the dollar's value. If you make rash decisions based on that information, you will be setting yourself up to miss your goals dramatically.

Additionally, the Internet can be a quagmire. Sure, you can surf your way to an abundance of fascinating information. You can pull down data and advice from a seemingly unlimited number of websites. Remember, however, that those online bloggers and other denizens of the World Wide Web have no knowledge of your situation. The data is for reference only, and it is up to you to determine its quality and validity. I use the Internet extensively in my work every day, but I know and respect the sources that I use. I know them to be level-headed and thoughtful.

My biggest problem with the Internet is that many websites seem to be huckstering for you to buy a subscription. You hear it on traditional media, as well: "Buy gold!" someone will be shouting at one time or another. And the next week: "Buy silver!" Sometimes it's the same voice exhorting you not to miss out on "the best investment possible."

That is a far cry from goals-based planning and investing. There is no way that one size can fit all, which is the impression that you would get from the media. The columnists, commentators, colleagues, friends, or relatives do not know your specific situation. Virtually everyone keeps both a private and a public persona. We rarely make public all of our wishes, concerns, and goals. Some things remain private, and we share them only with those whom we trust implicitly.

YOU'RE IN CONTROL

As I begin working with a new client and putting the financial plan in place, I open communications among the various team members, including the accountant and the estate attorney. During this time, the client is in charge, observing and participating to the extent desired. For the most part, the client communicates directly with me because I understand the overall scenario in a way that the individual experts do not.

I also understand the client personally in a way that those other individual experts do not. The clients have filled me in on the family dynamics. I understand the stresses that the couple faces as they deal with family issues and how these stresses can compound whenever finances are involved. I sometimes feel the tension between couples as they discuss financial matters in my office. Mostly they discuss disagreements in a playful manner, but beneath the surface, I can sense the friction. Money matters can drive a wedge between spouses. Usually the stress comes when the money is tight, but having too much money and multiple options can be stressful, too. In either case, thorough and timely communication is essential.

If you strive for an open and trusting relationship with your financial advisor, you will be on the right track. Someone who understands your situation and your dreams will be able to point to the most appropriate tools to achieve your goals. You maintain control, and you gain expertise along the way.

CHAPTER FIVE

RISKS AT EVERY TURN

I recently visited an eighty-four-year-old man whom a friend had suggested might require my services in managing his portfolio. He and his wife were in a continuous-care facility, and when I visited their apartment, he answered the door. I could see right away that his health was seriously impaired.

"My advisor is retiring," he explained, "and I'm looking for someone new to handle my accounts." We talked for a while—he told me about their son and two daughters—and then he began telling me in general terms about his financial situation and net worth. I listened intently, considering the best way that I might help, but he hadn't provided sufficient details to get very far.

"Let's take a look at your statements," I said. He had yet to bring anything out on the table. "To answer some of these questions, we need to do some planning."

"Planning?" he said, half smiling, as he adjusted his oxygen line. "I'm eighty-four years old! Just what would we be planning for?"

"I understand," I said, "but see, your wife is still very healthy, and we need to talk about various scenarios involving how long both you and she might live."

He did not seem willing to go down that road, but he did begin to express more clearly how he had been managing their finances. "We purchased some annuities so my wife will have a guaranteed income if I go first," he said.

And then he added: "And I have this other account—it's a million and a half dollars. I keep that under active management, and since my guy will be retiring, I figured that you might want the job."

I paused. "Okay, might I ask what it is actively managed in?"

"It's in individual stocks. They do a lot of trading—and these are high-quality securities, for sure." He seemed proud of his portfolio.

"Well, that's interesting," I began—and then I cut to the chase: "Look, this is probably where we're going to be parting ways."

"Why?"

"I'm not going to be trading individual stocks for you," I said. "In my opinion, it is inappropriate to be trading individual stocks for an elderly man in ill health."

"I don't understand why you would just put the kibosh on that," he said. "After all, I have all these annuities . . ."

"What you have," I said, "is a totally inappropriate strategy for someone your age. If you were to pass away, and at the same time the market pulled back 20 or 30 percent, your million and a half could turn into a million. And your son and daughters would understandably be marching in here to ask me, 'Why in the world were you trading individual stocks for our elderly father?'"

I needed to be frank with him. "That's why I can't help you. I don't know why your current advisor has been doing that. It's a tremendous liability for you. I wouldn't even consider managing your money unless your wife and at least one of your children were involved—but in any case, it's clear that you're looking for a kind of relationship that you wouldn't find with me."

And so we shook hands—a friendly but firm parting. My focus is on doing the right thing for people. There is no fee that will persuade me to do otherwise.

THREATS TO YOUR DREAMS

Most people, when they consider the risks that they face in their finances, think first of market risk. That certainly was the risk that the elderly gentleman was facing as he exposed much of his nest egg to the ebb and flow of individual stocks. Risk management, however, involves much more than the market, and it is a key function of a good financial advisor.

At every turn, retirees and soon-to-be retirees face threats to their financial well-being. If those threats come to pass and take their toll, the portfolio simply will not have decades to recover and grow anew. Mistakes made now have the potential to seriously affect retirees' lifestyles.

Risks come in many forms, besides the market. Take inflation, for example: What if inflation returns in double-digit doses? Many people of retirement age recall this happening when they were much younger. Even at a normal pace, inflation eats away at your nest egg. What if interest rates do not meet your expectations? Taxes, if managed incorrectly, can put your financial plan at risk of delivering less than expected. The possibility of illness and eventually needing long-term care are risks that must be addressed. Or you might live a long time and demand more of your portfolio than had been originally expected. Retirees are understandably concerned about outlasting their resources.

These are all risks that can seriously infringe upon your retirement dreams. But they can all be managed effectively when considered as part of an overall financial plan. We will examine some of those risks in this chapter. You will be reading about others, such as taxation and long-term care, in the chapters ahead.

MARKET RISK

Imagine yourself having just retired when you get some bad news from your doctor. You have a serious and chronic condition that is debilitating, although you could live for years with proper treatment and special care. You had not anticipated such a drain on your portfolio. To complicate matters, the market crashes, causing your investments to plunge in value. Scenarios like this one pose a real threat to even the best-laid plans.

I do not mean to be a harbinger of doom. Most couples enjoy many fruitful years in retirement. But let there be no doubt—what I previously described sometimes happens. If your retirement lifestyle is dependent on withdrawals from an account that fluctuates with the market, you are more or less at the mercy of the market. And as we all know or should know, the market can be 100 percent unpredictable. If your nest egg suffers a major hit early in retirement, and at the same time you face unforeseen expenses, your portfolio could spiral to the point where recovery is unlikely.

Even in a secular bull market, 10 percent corrections during the course of a year are considered to be normal. This means that you need to be cognizant of the timing of your capital needs, always considering the risk of market volatility. Unfortunately, you don't always know when you may face those needs. They can come at the worst time possible for you to tap into your savings.

To mitigate that risk, you should carry some assets in safer and more stable vehicles of moderate risk. That will give you flexibility in dealing with unknown expenses that spring up unexpectedly.

Market risk involves more than just plunging security values. If you don't need or have to withdraw the money, then the losses are simply on paper. The portfolio has the potential to rebound as the market recovers. Conversely, if you do require the money, it will matter significantly whether the bad years come earlier in your retirement or later. The sequence of returns will profoundly influence how much money remains in your portfolio.

For example, let's say that you retired in 1999 or early 2000 and faced three years straight of negative returns as the dot-com bubble burst. You then had no choice but to pull money out at the same time for living expenses. Your portfolio was highly vulnerable. Some of those who faced that scenario back then are running out of money today, when they are most vulnerable: in their late seventies or eighties, with little prospect of getting a job to make up for those losses.

I keep all that in mind while modeling portfolios and running projections for my clients. As we evaluate the risks, it is very important to discuss the concept of "winning by not losing." If you are invested in the market, you cannot always avoid losses, but you certainly can structure your financial plan and portfolio to mitigate risks and work toward sidestepping a significant amount of those losses.

In the market crash of 2008, some couples had to curtail their retirement dreams as they lost a major portion of their savings, or they had to keep plugging away on the job long after they had expected to be enjoying retirement. Others faced an entirely different kind of market risk: They succumbed to fear. The atmosphere of fear and stress caused an enormous amount of damage to portfolios. It led to the correlation of losses among different types of investments. By March 2009, many investors—particularly retired ones—had lost their trust in the markets. They stayed on the sidelines. They pulled their money out at the bottom and missed the recovery entirely.

Much has been written about the wisdom of investing in a direction opposite of your emotional inclinations as you observe what is happening in the market. When the financial media paint a bleak picture, it is typically a time to consider putting part of your portfolio where others might not dare.

As the renowned investor and philanthropist Sir John Templeton observed, "Bull markets are born on pessimism, grown on skepticism, mature on optimism, and die on euphoria." No one can deny that it is wise to buy low and sell high. Unfortunately, it is difficult to get the individual investor, especially the retired investor, to take profits during periods of euphoria or to enter the market during periods of panic. Ironically, they seem to want to buy other people's offerings at peak price and to sell their own at a bargain price. No other market works that way.

Nothing is new with regard to market cycles or human behavior. "We have nothing to fear but fear itself," Franklin D. Roosevelt proclaimed in his 1933 inaugural address, as the Great Depression took its toll. Nearly eight decades later, fear continued to trip people up. Like deer in headlights, people froze—and got hit hard. During these times, a trusted advisor is indispensable in making it through the storm.

The advisor also can assist in maintaining balance. The concept of *rebalancing* is critical to portfolio management. We regularly review the portfolios of each of our clients to make sure that they stay aligned with the clients' risk tolerance. You may have heard some advisors suggesting a balance of stocks and bonds in which the percentage of bonds is the same as your age. The presumption is that such a balance gives you a progressively more conservative investment as you get older. However, such a mix will not work in times of high fear, when the direction that stocks and bonds take can become highly correlated.

It is important to remember that different asset classes will perform in different ways and at different times in the market cycle, which is typically three to five years long. For example, at times, small-cap stocks will significantly outperform large caps. Let's say that for whatever reason, you would like to maintain a fifty–fifty mix of stocks and bonds. Over time, if your stocks have been performing well, you could find yourself with a portfolio that has migrated to a fifty-five/forty-five mix of stocks and bonds. Ideally, you want the portfolio to stay true to the original asset allocation. To rebalance, we would need to research your best performers on the equity side. If we identified that the small-cap investments were responsible for a large portion of growth, we could decide to move that portion of the gain over to bonds. The goal is to sell securities that are at or near their high, rather than selling off pieces that have declined significantly in value. It's a matter of staying on track—methodically adjusting the portfolio to sell high and buy low.

INFLATION RISK

For the retiree concerned about losing money, inflation is unlikely to be the first threat that comes to mind. That is because inflation is insidious. It worms into your portfolio over the years and erodes it. A decade passes, and retirees notice that their fixed income no longer meets their living expenses.

One of the first questions that I ask clients when we regularly meet is whether they have been feeling comfortable with their cash flow and expenses each month. As the years go by, cash flow gets tighter. Pension payments usually don't increase, and Social Security increases are intermittent. Meanwhile, fixed expenses and discretionary items become more expensive. If I hear that a client is starting to feel pinched, I say that it's time to turn on the faucet. We need to discuss drawing more of an income from the portfolio.

Inflation can inflict much harm. It is hard on everyone's portfolio, but it is particularly hard on the portfolios of retirees on fixed incomes that face inflationary pressures unique to their age group. The Bureau of Labor Statistics issues a separate inflation number for retirees, and it tends to be higher than the general inflation rate. That is because expenses such as health care, medications, and food, which are prominent line items on retirees' budgets, tend to increase more than the other expenses.

To keep up with inflation, a financial plan needs to allow for enough growth over time to keep up with inflation. Typically, that growth will be derived from some level of equity exposure. Generally, inflation will be higher at the same time that interest rates are higher. Therefore, when you look at the return rate on your CD or bond, what you really need to consider is the net return after inflation. Currently, the net return after inflation on a seven- or ten-year US Treasury note is less than half a percent, without accounting for taxation.

The chart below details the erosion of purchasing power specifically for older Americans. It illustrates a comparison between the inflation experienced by an older individual (CPI-E) versus

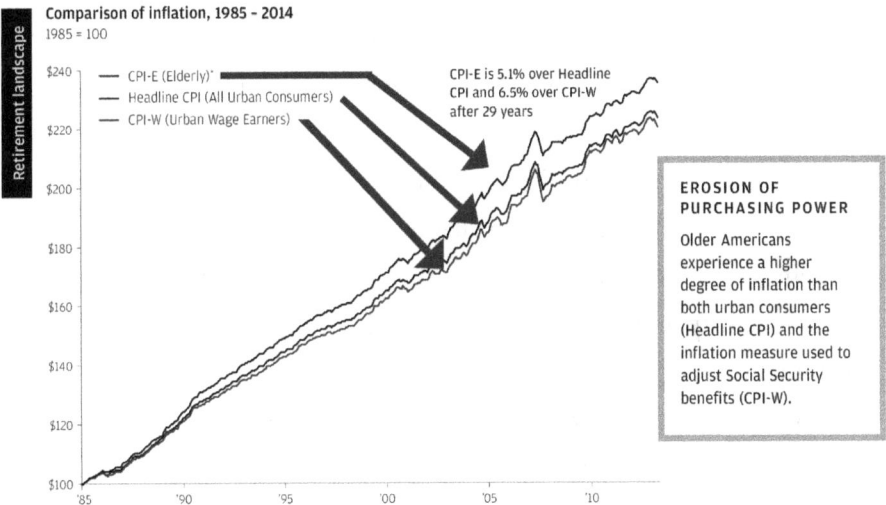

Older individuals experience higher inflation

Comparison of inflation, 1985 - 2014
1985 = 100

Retirement landscape

— CPI-E (Elderly)*
— Headline CPI (All Urban Consumers)
— CPI-W (Urban Wage Earners)

CPI-E is 5.1% over Headline CPI and 6.5% over CPI-W after 29 years

EROSION OF PURCHASING POWER

Older Americans experience a higher degree of inflation than both urban consumers (Headline CPI) and the inflation measure used to adjust Social Security benefits (CPI-W).

J.P.Morgan
Asset Management

*CPI-E is an experimental index from BLS that is based on elderly households with the referenced individuals at age 62 and older. Source: Based on Consumer Price Indexes, BLD, J.P. Morgan Asset Management. Data as of December 31, 2014.

the inflation experienced by urban consumers (CPI-U or Headline CPI) and the index used to inflate the cost-of-living adjustments for Social Security (CPI-W). Clearly, older Americans experience a higher degree of inflation over time—outpacing the general inflation measure as well as the rate at which Social Security increases over time.

INTEREST RATE RISK

If you think back to the days of 13 percent CD rates, you may recall that those were also the days when inflation was nearly that high. One reason for the recent low interest rates has been the recent low inflation rates, calculated by the Federal Reserve at 1.5 to 1.6 percent annually. The Fed generally has raised interest rates to ease inflationary pressures in the economy.

Imagine if you had pinned your retirement hopes on the high interest rates that once were available. Half a million dollars at 13 percent annually is an income of $65,000 a year, and along with Social Security and pension, you would be set for a lifetime—or so you might have thought.

Whether you are dealing with CDs or bonds, the question is this: When they come due, and what interest rate can you get when you reinvest? In 2008, you could get 4 to 5 percent interest on a CD. Today, a five-year CD is averaging 1.2 to 1.5 percent.[6] To put that in perspective, it means that in 2008, a $100,000 CD would have drawn about $4,500 in income. In 2015, that same investment, at 1.25 percent, would produce only $1,250 a year.

---

6 "CD rates history," Bankrate, Accessed on February 11, 2016, http://www.bankrate.com/finance/cd-rates-history-0112.aspx.

Meanwhile, inflation has continued to erode your resources. After inflation and taxes, it's possible that you will have no net return.

That, in essence, demonstrates interest rate risk. It generally is a term applied to bond investments: as interest rates rise, bond prices fall as investors pursue the opportunity for a greater gain elsewhere. Likewise, as interest rates fall, bonds become more attractive because of their fixed rate and increase in value. Bond investors are on a seesaw and must be aware of rising interest rates that might damage their portfolio.

THE RISK OF LONGEVITY

Today's retirees need to deal with the fact that there could be decades of years ahead of them. Perhaps the greatest risk of all is that of outliving your financial resources. The decisions that you make during your working years will have a huge impact on your ability to retire comfortably and maintain your lifestyle throughout retirement.

The IRS figures that you will last quite some time: its schedule for distributions from retirement accounts takes you almost to age one hundred. That's a long time that your nest egg must provide for you. And with increased longevity, the cost of long-term care inevitably must enter into the equation, whether it is self-funded or paid with annual insurance premiums. None of us want to be a burden on our families or on society.

It is critical to find a trusted advisor who will help you assess all of the factors and risks that play into your financial-planning approach. It is absolutely essential to understand the full picture of your expenses, debts, goals, and dreams. Only then can we see the most appropriate ways to address the variety of risks that every retiree faces and prepare a plan for the many good years ahead.

CHAPTER SIX

MANAGING THE TAXES

I n 2004, I began working with the clients of another financial advisor, who was retiring. Many of the clients' assets were tied up in IRAs, which posed its own set of challenges. For example, to avoid the tax hit of an IRA withdrawal, the previous advisor had been suggesting alternative methods to finance major purchases, such as obtaining as large a mortgage as possible to buy a vacation home.

One couple, who had dreamed of having a lake house in the mountains, had taken his advice in 1999. Instead of withdrawing money from their IRA, they obtained the money for a down payment by taking out a second mortgage on their primary residence. They then secured a mortgage for the lake house, with 100 percent financing. The new debt was $300,000.

The couple's portfolio had increased dramatically in the previous five years, rising from around $400,000 to about a million dollars. This was followed by several difficult years in the market, causing a significant loss in the portfolio at the same time that they were expected to continue the existing mortgage payments and maintenance expenses on the property.

Four years later, when I began working with them, their net worth had fallen by 60 percent. Their portfolio was back down to $400,000, and their lifestyle had diminished significantly. I worked with them to figure out strategies just to meet expenses.

By that point, they had ceased traveling, other than to the lake house. But despite the financial stress, they did share many good memories with family, including summer visits from the grandchildren. The wife eventually passed away, and in 2010, the lake house went back on the market. It sold for only $20,000 more than the couple had paid for it eleven years earlier.

I cannot help but think how much better that expense could have been handled at the outset. In 1999, no one knew that the market was about to collapse, but a look back at the couple's portfolio would have clearly indicated its impressive growth in the previous five years. Their advisor had done well for them. However, ten years into retirement, the couple found themselves with a nest egg equal to what it had been in 1994.

Additionally, they had a large mortgage on an illiquid investment. To avoid tax consequences, they had decided not to withdraw a lump sum from their IRA to pay for the lake house. Instead, they heeded their financial planner's advice to fully finance the purchase.

Consider how the situation might have looked if they had paid cash for the house. After paying the $300,000 in purchase costs and taxes, they would have had about $600,000 left in their account, and they would have owned the house free and clear. No withdrawals would have been required from their portfolio, and they would have been far better positioned to endure the upcoming market crisis.

This is not traditional tax wisdom. But in this couple's situation, it could have been the best thing to do. The lesson is this: Every situation needs to be examined and projected. Blanket policies such as "never do this" or "always do that" may be based on general truths, but they fail to take into account your personal circumstances.

When it comes to saving on taxes, a look at the entire picture often reveals that the real problem is a steady drain on finances that, in time, can amount to a fortune. Often it is not some major tax situation that inflicts the pain. Rather, it comes slowly and incessantly over many years.

When we analyze our clients' taxes and examine their returns, we often see methods by which we can prevent taxes from being paid unnecessarily. In doing so, we take a look at the type of investments and where they are located, such as within a 401(k), an IRA, or a taxable account. The more you can save on taxes, the more money you will have to distribute at your own discretion. Instead of the government deciding who gets your tax dollars, you can choose to direct those dollars to family or to the charities of your choosing.

TAX TREATMENT OF INVESTMENTS

Most people are aware that different investments come with different tax treatments, which can play a major role in portfolio management. When saving for retirement, many people keep a mix of taxable, tax-free, and tax-deferred investments. Let's take a look at each of those three categories.

TAXABLE

These are the normal investments on which taxes are paid in the same year in which income is realized. Taxable accounts include individual stocks that have gains or losses, dividends paid on those stocks, certificates of deposit, corporate and US government bonds, and mutual funds.

Mutual funds can generate what is known as *phantom income tax*. This occurs when you are purchasing the fund outside of a tax-deferred account. For example, suppose your mutual fund buys a stock at $100 a share, and it increases to $200 a share. You buy into the fund after the stock appreciates. If the mutual fund manager decides to sell all or part of that stock position, any gains over the original cost basis are distributed to each shareholder on a per-share basis. Therefore, you can find yourself in a position of owing tax on capital gain even though you personally saw none of the appreciation. In fact, you might have seen an overall loss on your fund investment and still owe tax. That's why it is known as phantom tax, but it is very real. You and your planner must be cognizant of that potential whenever buying a mutual fund in a taxable environment.*

*Investors should consider the investment objectives, risks, and charges and expenses of mutual funds and exchange-traded funds carefully before investing. The prospectus contains this and other information about mutual funds and exchange–traded funds. The prospectus is available from your financial advisor and should be read carefully before investing.

TAX-FREE

This category of investment and account types includes municipal bonds, Roth IRA's, certain insurance product loans and 529 education accounts.

- Municipal bonds issued in localities around the country are generally considered to be tax-free. Taxable bonds are sometimes issued, but those tend to involve partnerships that the municipality has in conjunction with for-profit companies and organizations. However, the interest income derived from school district bonds and general obligation bonds of a municipality are not taxed.[7]

- A Roth IRA—a retirement account to which you contribute after-tax dollars—will allow you, under current regulations, with some restrictions, to withdraw your money tax-free. This applies to the total amount contributed or to the amount that the money has grown.[8]

- Likewise, your contributions to a 529 education account also generally are made with after-tax dollars. You can withdraw the money for qualified expenses such as

7 Municipal bond interest is not subject to federal income tax but may be subject to AMT, state, or local taxes. Income from taxable municipal bonds is subject to federal-income taxation, and it may be subject to state and local taxes. Municipal securities typically provide a lower yield than comparably rated taxable investments in consideration of their tax-advantaged status. Investments in municipal securities may not be appropriate for all investors, particularly those who do not stand to benefit from the tax status of the investment. Please consult an income-tax professional to assess the impact of holding such securities on your tax liability
8 Unless certain criteria are met, Roth IRA owners must be fifty-nine and a half or older and have held the IRA for five years before tax-free withdrawals are permitted.

tuition, room and board, books, or required technological equipment such as a computer. Distributions of any growth on the investment are tax-free. However, if you take a nonqualified distribution, you face significant consequences: income tax is paid on the growth, plus a 10 percent penalty.

- If you structure a life insurance policy properly, such as whole life or universal life, and have funded it with a significant amount of after-tax money over the years, you can withdraw the cash value via a policy loan.[9]

TAX-DEFERRED

In the tax-deferred arena, the vehicle with which most people are familiar, particularly if they work for a for-profit organization, is the 401(k). If you are employed by a nonprofit organization, it is typically a 403(b). They work similarly, with a few differences in regulations.

The amount that you (as an employee) contribute to such a plan each year is not immediately subjected to income tax. Rather, the tax is deferred throughout your working years until you withdraw the money from the account—presumably during retirement.[10] At that point, every withdrawal will generate a 1099 and will be

9 When you take out a loan against your life insurance policy (except a modified endowment contract, or MEC), the amount you receive is not considered taxable income. If you cancel your policy while there is a loan balance outstanding, you could be subject to income tax on the amount of the loan (plus any accrued but unpaid interest). Be sure to contact a qualified professional regarding your particular situation before initiating a policy loan.
10 Withdrawals are subject to income taxes and, if withdrawn prior to age fifty-nine and a half, may also be subject to a 10 percent federal penalty

taxable income. Some 401(k) plans include a Roth option, whereby you can also contribute after-tax money that you will be able to withdraw later, tax-free.

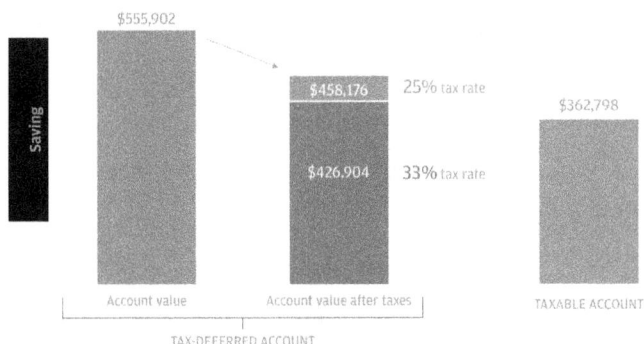

The power of tax-deferred compounding

Taxable vs. tax-deferred investing over a 30-year timeframe

Saving

$555,902

$458,176   25% tax rate

$426,904   33% tax rate

$362,798

Account value   Account value after taxes

TAX-DEFERRED ACCOUNT

TAXABLE ACCOUNT

ASSET LOCATION

Tax-advantaged accounts can shelter income-producing investments from current income taxation and result in greater long-term growth than taxable accounts.

J.P.Morgan
Asset Management

Source: J.P. Morgan Asset Management. Assumes $5,500 after-tax contributions at the beginning of each year for 30 years and 7% annual investment return. Tax-deferred account balance is taken as lump sum and taxed at the 25% and 33% federal tax rate, respectively, at time of withdrawal. Taxable account contributions are after-tax and assume a 33% federal tax rate during accumulation. This hypothetical illustration is not indicative of any specific investment and does not reflect the impact of fees or expenses. This chart is shown for illustrative purposes only. Past performance is no guarantee of future results.

Early withdrawals from tax-deferred accounts are subject to income taxes and, if withdrawn prior to age 59½, may also be subject to a 10% federal penalty. Every investor's situation is unique and you should consider your investment goals, risk tolerance, tax bracket, and time horizon before making any investment. Investing involves risk and you may incur a profit or loss regardless of strategy selected. Future performance cannot be guaranteed and investment yields will fluctuate with market conditions.

IRAs are quite similar to the 401(k), although the government, not the employer, sets the contribution limit. There are various types that you may have heard about: Simplified Employee Pension (SEP), IRAs and Savings Incentive Match Plan for Employees (SIMPLE), and IRAs for small employers and self-employed people. Like the 401(k), these programs are funded through contributions of pretax money, either as regular contributions or as an annual lump sum.

You also can purchase a tax-deferred annuity with after-tax money. You will pay no tax until the time of distribution. At that point, IRS regulations require the withdrawal of the growth portion before your contribution portion. In other words, the after-tax money is first in and last out, and the growth money is last in and first out.

Tax-deferred annuities come in many forms. They can be bare bones with lower expenses—purely for investment. They are designed specifically as tax-deferred vehicles during your working years, when wages and taxes are higher. Money can be put into a tax-deferred annuity outside of your 401(k), and all growth can be shielded from tax until withdrawn later in life. Variable tax-deferred annuities, which have a variety of investment options (called sub-accounts), are also available. Or you can have a tax-deferred annuity with a fixed rate. Please remember that Variable Annuities are long term investments designed specifically for retirement purposes.[11]

---

11 All guarantees are subject to the claims-paying ability of the issuing insurance company, which is solely responsible for obligations under its contracts. Withdrawals will generally be subject to a surrender penalty if redeemed during the surrender-charge period and if they are in excess of any free withdrawal provisions. Since annuities grow tax-deferred, any withdrawals made prior to age fifty-nine and a half may be subject to a 10 percent federal tax penalty in addition to any gains being taxed as ordinary income.

ZERO CAPITAL GAINS TAX

An interesting aspect of the current tax code is that if you are in the lowest tax bracket for ordinary income, you do not have to pay the tax on long-term capital gains or on qualified dividends.

The 15 percent tax bracket, for taxable income after deductions, goes up to $37,450 for an individual and to $74,900 for a married couple filing jointly. Therefore, a retired couple with $80,000–$90,000 or more in gross income may still fall into the 15 percent bracket after their deductions. This makes them eligible to pay zero tax on dividends and long-term capital gains.

We pay close attention to these margins. Sometimes, it can be difficult to keep clients within the lower bracket if most of their assets are in a 401(k) or an IRA, and they must take out large distributions when they turn seventy-and-a-half years old. We try to manage their accounts to compensate for that. We examine their tax returns and work with accountants and tax attorneys to determine how much income or capital gains they can have before getting pushed into a higher bracket.

While we closely monitor and analyze the tax situation, some years can still provide surprises. This can be the result of the distributions generated by investments during the last quarter of the year. These distributions can be present even in a year in which the investor lost money on the fund and can generate the phantom tax mentioned earlier. That is an inherent difficulty when investing in investments outside of a tax-deferred account. Even with consistent monitoring, unexpected distributions can disrupt the calculations for remaining within the lower tax bracket.

A CLOSER LOOK AT RETIREMENT PLANS

The principle behind tax-deferred investments is that you will have more money growing over the years, and ostensibly, that would mean that you will have a lot more in your account by the time you retire.

Some advisors ask whether that might be an exercise in futility. Instead, they suggest, people should opt to put after-tax money away in a Roth IRA or a tax-deferred annuity. Today's relatively low tax rate, it is noted, means that we may be facing higher rates in the future, particularly with the large deficits that the government has been running. In other words, a tax-deferred investment could actually be deferring to a higher tax rate rather than a lower one. Would it not be better to pay the tax at today's rate and not be concerned about how high it might be down the road?

My concern is that the government could decide to change the rules on Roth IRAs and Roth 401(k)s. If the government is trying to drum up more money, changing the rules is a distinct possibility. As such, the argument in favor of the Roth accounts is not as strong as it might seem to some. Additionally, the traditional plans are not just pre-income tax but are also prepayroll taxes—there are no FICA, Social Security, or Medicare taxes on those dollars, either. The taxes continue to be avoided even after withdrawing those dollars in retirement.

Traditional plans help you to avoid a significant percentage of taxes. People who are in their thirties or forties today and are earning an average income are more likely to be paying at a higher tax rate now than they will when they are retired. Through the years, we have been able to work with our clients' accountants and tax attorneys to produce a much lower effective tax rate and maintain a much lower tax bracket during retirement.

At retirement, assets must be properly distributed among taxable, tax-deferred, and tax-free vehicles. If most of your assets are in a traditional 401(k) or IRA, we need to determine whether it would be wise to begin withdrawing some income prior to age seventy and a half, when your distributions must begin, to help reduce larger outflows of taxable income later.

It is also important to consider what you will do with those proceeds. If you are required to make a withdrawal but do not require the money for living expenses, this could be an opportunity to review whether you wish to assist your adult children. If you withdraw the money, pay the tax, and put it back into taxable investments, you will effectively be paying taxes twice. You need to look at tax-efficient investments, which could include municipal bonds, individual dividend-paying stocks, or exchange-traded funds.

All of this depends on the specific nature of your finances and your situation. To make the proper decisions, you and your financial advisor need to look at all facets of the tax picture. The best course of action is always on a case-by-case basis. This is an ideal time to work closely with your advisor to make important decisions on how you intend to use the money.

We believe that it is crucial to save continuously. The major advantage of retirement plans is that they acclimate people to the discipline of systematic saving. For many, investing systematically is done out of sight and out of mind. The money is automatically drafted from each paycheck and distributed to the desired investment choices. This is particularly important for moderate- to lower-income families during their working years. If they can learn to live without a portion of their income, they will be pleasantly surprised at how their account grows. With this systematic contribution, they are invoking the principle of *dollar cost averaging*. By buying on a regular schedule, they attain a lower cost over time through ongoing price fluctuations in their desired securities. They tend to buy more shares at a lower price and fewer at a higher price.[12]

Some employers provide a match for employee contributions, and that is a big advantage. Matching and profit-sharing opportunities should not be overlooked. A lot of smaller companies set up what is called a *safe harbor match*. The safe harbor match provides 3 percent of each employee's salary to the plan every year, whether the employee contributes to the plan or not. For employees making just $30,000 a year, that's $900 a year. Additionally, if they can put $900, or 3 percent, of their own salary in, they are effectively investing $900 of their own money and automatically getting another $900 from the company. That is a 100 percent return on investment. Companies can also institute profit sharing on a discretionary basis, but the company match is what we see most often.

For years I have worked closely with a company that employs a lot of young, single mothers. We have shown them the importance of saving their own money and of receiving the company match and profit sharing. I have a long history with these employees, and I can see what they have been able to accomplish. A few years ago, they had nothing saved, but some of them now have almost $15,000 in their respective accounts. It is a lot more than they previously had thought was possible.

---

12 Dollar-cost averaging cannot guarantee a profit or protect against a loss, and you should consider your financial ability to continue purchases through periods of low price levels.

Systematic savings, with the money regularly withdrawn from paychecks, helps to overcome the human tendency to spend whatever is available. For the employees, it builds a sense of confidence that they could change their existing situation for the better. The employers gain a sense of loyalty from their employees. Most readers of this book, as well as my clients, have reached a position in life far more affluent than these young people struggling to find their way. I believe that my industry must make a commitment to assist all people in becoming financially astute.

STRETCH PROVISIONS

IRAs offer a generational advantage that should be considered as part of a family's financial planning. A 401(k) can be rolled over into an IRA and then structured in such a way that it can be passed on to children or other designated beneficiaries while continuing to be stretched out over their lifetimes.

We have found that many clients, following retirement, still live frugally and generally take out only the required minimum distribution from their retirement accounts. If they do not live to their full life expectancy, their retirement accounts are often left with a rather large pool of capital. Establishing a stretch provision maintains the tax deferral on the asset base for another generation, which provides for a significant amount of additional growth for the heirs. In effect, it can provide a supplemental pension for their children's retirement needs.

An extremely important aspect of an IRA is the beneficiary designation. If the beneficiary form is not filled out correctly and the beneficiary is listed as the estate of the deceased, then all monies have to come out of the retirement account in one year, and the estate has to pay income tax on it. That is a big problem. A lump sum distribution can lose 40 percent or more of the value of the account immediately. Families need to be extremely careful how the account passes on to the next generation. Children should encourage their parents to keep the beneficiary form updated.

For many people, the largest asset besides their home is their 401(k) or other retirement plan. This needs to be managed with wisdom. A major part of that wisdom involves thorough communication. The beneficiary is not required to accept the stretch provision. He or she can always elect to take the lump sum, either in a single year or in a few equal payments. The tax and growth benefits of stretching the account out over the beneficiary's life expectancy can be significant, but this is optional.

That is why it is important to make sure that your children or other heirs understand your intentions with regard to the inherited funds. If they see that your desire is to provide a continuing income for future generations, they may be less inclined to splurge on a depreciating material asset.

YOUR FAIR SHARE

"Fair share" is in the eye of the beholder. I know people who don't seem to flinch at paying higher tax rates, and I know others who make high incomes and find the 28 percent or the 39.6 percent federal tax brackets to be quite discouraging. An important aspect of financial planning is not only to put the long-term preparations in place but also to look at the annual tax implications of your decisions on your portfolio. You should be looking for any tax relief that is legally available to you.

Why does the government offer tax breaks? How can it be in the government's best interest to give people relief when it comes to paying taxes? Why would it give a break to charities and the people who give to charities?

Charities do a tremendous amount of community work, whether it is feeding the poor or researching cures for diseases. It is in the best interest of society that this type of work continues, and a government serving said society will want to advance those interests. Tax breaks are an incentive to do work that the government would otherwise need to fund with tax dollars.

I know someone quite well who has multiple sclerosis, and the MS Society provides a tremendous amount of financial support for research on this chronic disease. It is a fund-raising charity that raises capital for a worthy cause, and the government recognizes that. In short, the government uses tax breaks to encourage behaviors deemed worthwhile. For example, it encourages research, home ownership, and a variety of other pursuits.

The government will not go out of its way to inform you of these tax breaks. You need to research and discover them for yourself. It is unlikely that a stockbroker will point out the tax implications, either. You should be working with a financial advisor and tax accountant whose allegiances are squarely with you. They can advise you on how you can organize your accounts for the greatest tax advantage.

A good financial advisor takes a holistic view of your family's financial affairs and develops a solid understanding of your needs and desires. Among those many considerations are the tax obligations that must be paid. Your advisor and tax accountant should help you to determine the best strategy to ensure tax efficiency while freeing up as much money as possible for the pursuits that you deem worthy.

CHAPTER SEVEN

IN SICKNESS AND HEALTH

Most of my clients desire to leave a legacy to their heirs. Generally, their heirs are their children. A major concern is the prospect of the client needing long-term care for a debilitating illness such as Alzheimer's, which can last for years and reduce any potential inheritance.

Long-term care insurance is not for everyone. If you are able to self-finance, that's fine. But if your estate is worth less than $1 million, consider the cost of long-term care. The median annual rate for a semiprivate room at a long-term care facility is now $80,300, and a private room currently costs $91,250, according to a 2015 cost-of-care survey by Genworth Financial.[13] It is unlikely, if you have $600,000 or $700,000 in savings, that you can afford that expense while also having much of a bequest for your heirs.

The public generally has little knowledge of how the Medicare and Medicaid systems function when it comes to long-term care. Medicare provides only limited and relatively brief coverage, with strict conditions. Medicaid contributes to cover the bills for those who have become destitute. To become eligible for Medicaid, you need to meet your state's income eligibility requirement, which might be set at any level up to 133 percent of the federal poverty level. If you have resources available to pay for the care, you will be expected to use most of those resources prior to being considered for Medicaid.

When designing a solution for long-term care, it is important to have a financial planner and an elder-care attorney working with you to assist in protecting assets. In one case, a client who for years had adamantly refused to consider long-term care insurance found that he needed to enter a nursing home. He eventually spent his life savings down to $20,000. We then brought in an elder-care attorney for the transition to Medicaid coverage, but the client passed away.

Long-term care insurance can come in a variety of forms, and it is all part of the comprehensive planning required by retirees to address the many issues that they face. Needing long-term care can significantly influence the outcome of the financial plan. It can devastate a portfolio.

People often are reluctant to deal with this crucial issue. They procrastinate because addressing the topic raises the subject of their

13   https://www.genworth.com/dam/Americas/US/PDFs/Consumer/corporate/130568_040115_gnw.pdf.

own mortality. They don't want to be a burden on their children. Nonetheless, they need to candidly discuss the prospect that the day will come when they cannot handle their own affairs. I have noticed that people in their late seventies become more willing to discuss long-term care. In their more vibrant years, people tend to feel that it is unlikely that they will ever be in that situation. Those who have witnessed someone that they love reach the point of needing long-term care are more likely to appreciate the importance of preparing for it. They would like to spare their own children some of the heartache that can come with a long, debilitating illness.

TRADITIONAL LONG-TERM CARE INSURANCE

My parents purchased traditional long-term care insurance in 1991, when the industry was in its infancy. It was a policy that provided for benefits with an inflation ratchet. In my parents' case, my father had paid premiums of roughly $2,800 a year from 1991 through 2004. He was diagnosed with pancreatic cancer and died eight months later, never using the policy.

In their case, the financial risk amounted to about $36,000. My father never derived any benefit from it. This remains a major reason that some people resist traditional insurance. They don't want to be spending a significant amount of money on premiums if there is no benefit to them—but there is a benefit. They are purchasing reassurance that they will be covered in the event that something does happen. Nonetheless, they know that they will never get those premiums back.

Traditional long-term care insurance is similar to car insurance. If you don't use it, you lose it. You pay a premium, either monthly, quarterly, semiannually, or annually. Your policy generally provides for a daily benefit and can have many riders.

The older you become, the more expensive the long-term care policy becomes. Under current policy guidelines, most insurance companies can opt to raise premiums. I have seen them increase as much as 7 to 15 percent per year. That's a significant increase for someone on a fixed income. My mother, for example, is still paying the premiums on her policy, twenty-four years later. She has paid out a significant amount of money, and at age eighty-two, she has no desire to cancel the policy. The premiums, which were originally $2,800, are now running close to $4,400 annually. This increase of premium can affect the lifestyle of retirees on a fixed income.

None of this means that traditional insurance policies for long-term care are a bad thing. When considering such a policy, you must understand not only the immediate expenses and benefits but also the potential costs of paying the premium for many years and possibly never needing the care.

ASSET-BASED POLICIES

As an alternative, asset-based long-term care policies are essentially life insurance policies with a very low death benefit and a long-term care rider. In many instances, you can pay either a single premium or spread the payments out over as long as ten years. You choose a desired premium amount based on the coverage amounts that you are most likely to need.

For example, you decide to put in $30,000 over a decade. That's $3,000 a year, and that premium never goes up during that time. You know ahead of time how much you will pay and what benefits are included. The benefit will be based on how much money has been paid as well as the pace at which you paid it. The benefit at, for example, age eighty-five will be much higher if the entire $30,000 premium was paid at the outset rather than in installments over ten years.

In either case, you define your input costs and get a defined-output benefit. For example, you might receive five years' worth of care benefits. According to Life Care Funding, a life insurance company based in Portland, Maine, an individual that requires skilled nursing-home care typically has a life expectancy of approximately thirty months.[14] An advantage of an asset-based policy is that it also includes a death benefit in the event that the provision is never needed. Typically, the death benefit is 150 percent to 200 percent of the initial deposit. If you put $30,000 in, your family might get back $45,000 to $60,000. While that is not a particularly high benefit, the asset was not lost to the estate. It's not a case of "use it or lose it."

SELF-INSURING AND CONTINUOUS CARE

If you do have sufficient financial resources, you can take the approach of budgeting funds to cover the costs of long-term care. Some affluent people reason that once they are in a nursing home, their other costs of living will be much lower. With their limited activities, their financial plan will be in a better position to absorb the monthly expense of long-term care.

Others reason like this: "I am going to live in my home for as long as I can, and I also will get in-home care for as long as I can. I

---

14 Chris Orestis, "Life Expectancy Compression: The impact of moving into a long term care facility on length of life," Life Care Funding, February 12, 2013, http://www.lifecarefunding.com/white-papers/moving-into-long-term-care-facility/.

will pay for this through my savings, and if at some point I cannot stay in my home and must move into a facility, then at that point, my home can be sold. The money from the sale will then provide for my long-term care expenses."

Continuous-care facilities are another way of self-insuring, and many such facilities are available in communities across the country. Typically, a couple will move into such a facility while they still are healthy and living independently. As they age, the community will provide assisted-living or full-skilled care.

At a continuous-care facility, you pay a rather large up-front cost upon moving in. This is a matter that should be discussed early on as you work with your advisor on preparing a financial plan. Anticipating that at some point you would like to move into a continuous-care facility is another good reason to ensure that you are no longer carrying a mortgage.

The capital gained from the sale of your house should be sufficient to fund the up-front cost of getting into a continuous-care facility. You will also face a monthly expense for living there, but you will no longer have a mortgage balance. Many people find that their Social Security benefit, pension, and portfolio income are more than enough to cover the monthly expense.

In addition, you will get a rather large tax deduction during the year of your move. About 40 percent of the initial deposit to enter a continuous-care facility is allocated toward the health care that you would receive there. The facility provides you with an end-of-the-year tax document breaking down the tax deduction.

Whether you self-insure or obtain some sort of policy to cover the expenses of long-term care is a decision that will depend upon your individual circumstances. As with other aspects of financial planning, there is no formula that works for everyone. Each family has differing needs, resources, and attitudes. What is clear is that addressing long-term care well in advance is crucial to protecting your life savings and avoiding the heartache that can result from inaction and uncertainty.

CHAPTER EIGHT

WINNING BY NOT LOSING

"When I die," a client once told me, "I want to be sure that my wife will be a rich old lady." I smiled, but I fully understood his sentiment. His approach was derived from love. He wanted to ensure that the flow of income through their retirement years would be sufficient and that if his wife became a widow, she would enjoy the lifestyle of their dreams. He would still be providing for her.

In working with individuals and couples to plan their retirement income needs, it is necessary to balance a variety of considerations. One of them is the concept of *financial risk tolerance*. By that, I mean not only how much risk you can mentally accept but also how much risk your portfolio can accept and still accomplish what is necessary. Most people want to see their portfolio grow more rapidly if possible.

The approach that I try to impress upon people is to "win by not losing." That means not losing at all, if possible. Or it can mean not losing significantly during the down years of the market. During economic slumps, the less you lose, the easier it will be to recoup losses and get back into positive territory.

HOW MUCH CAN YOU WITHDRAW?

Many have weighed in on what might be the proper percentage of annual withdrawal from a portfolio. That will depend, of course, on individual circumstances, but in my experience, a withdrawal rate of between 3 and 4 percent tends to be optimal for a couple entering retirement (depending upon their age). If a couple in their mid to late seventies is withdrawing a bit more, I'm not as concerned. Younger retirees, however, should stay in the 3 percent range.

If your financial planning indicates that you could do well with only a 3 percent withdrawal rate from your portfolio every year, you might be inclined to think that you should be taking on more risk and growing your portfolio to greater heights so that you can leave your heirs a larger bequest. You might tell yourself that you are doing pretty well at the moment, leading you to question if there is room for more risk.

Answering that question requires projection of expenses far beyond the immediate. How will you be doing in your more vulnerable years, when you are in your seventies and older? If you run out of money, will you be able to seek employment? Even if you are physically and mentally capable, will anyone hire you? If you need help around the house or someone to provide basic care, can you afford it? The vulnerable years are when issues and expenses can rise rapidly. In helping you with your financial planning, I want to ensure that you will be well positioned when you get to that point in your life.

To analyze cash-flow requirements, we must determine how much your portfolio needs to generate for you annually. In some years the market will do well, and in others it will perform poorly. This much is certain: no one has a crystal ball to predict just when those years will come.

If you retired in 2007, for example, and all your money was in the S&P 500 index, you would have lost a little over 38 percent of your portfolio value by December 31, 2008. Let's say that you also took out 3 percent for living expenses prior to that year's economic crisis. The following year, your losses would have required you to take out 4.8 percent from what remained of your portfolio to maintain your income level. That's simple math. On the other hand, if you were able to maintain investments that generated 4.5 percent annual return throughout the decade from 2000 to 2010, you would have outperformed the S&P 500 on an average basis during that period.

The key is to mitigate risk so that you do not absorb all of the market's downturns and are able to maintain reliable income during your retirement. To suffer a financial punch early in retirement does not necessarily mean that you will be destitute in the immediate future. But fast-forward ten or fifteen years, and your situation could be tenuous. You could eventually run out of money, and your problem would have its roots in what occurred, market-wise, when you first retired. To avoid running out of money, it is important to position your assets so that you participate in the up markets and try to mute the impact of the downturns.

This is what I mean when I say "winning by not losing." Though you cannot guarantee against a loss, properly diversified portfolios are designed so that your livelihood and lifestyle are not at the mercy of the markets. As I work with clients to develop income plans, we look to generate the lowest rate of return that will bring in enough money to meet their standard of living and their hopes for the future.

BUDGETING AND STRESS TESTING

To find out whether your financial plan can meet expectations, we subject it to various stress tests before considering individual investments. We begin with your existing resources and income sources. Following that, we figure in your needs, goals, and dreams. Lastly, we examine extensive possibilities and probabilities. We see how much your plan can bear. We then assess, analyze, and adjust based on historical data and project them into future scenarios.

We also budget. In my early conversations, I ask clients for a copy of their budget. Usually, they will come up with a breakdown of about ten budget items for me to review. They detail how much they are paying for utilities, cable TV, auto expenses, and so on. Then I look further: How much is their car insurance premium? What do they pay in property taxes?

Are they providing financial assistance to any of their children at the moment? Sometimes couples might actually forget about the help that they have been providing for a family member, or they may not consider it a budget expense. They might be somewhat embarrassed and not want to discuss it. But if they have been providing several thousand dollars annually for a family member, their financial plan can be significantly affected.

Automobiles can be a large expense item, too. How often are they replaced? Is it every five years? Ten years? What are the monthly and annual totals for automobile expenses? Is there a desire to travel? Occasionally, one spouse wants to travel, and the other is less enthusiastic about the idea. Nonetheless, money must be allocated appropriately. We discuss the cost of home repairs. Is there a wedding coming up? Often, people in their sixties still have children who are not yet married, and they hope to participate in the festivities. They also expect to participate in the expenses. A twenty-four-year-old daughter might not have a significant other at the moment, but a wedding expense still might be forthcoming within several years. We can figure that into the budget and take inflation into account.

As we budget, we research thoroughly to ensure that we have a complete listing of the expenses that we know will be coming up. We also anticipate unexpected life events, which helps to reduce anxiety when such expenses come along.

Having projected the likely expenses, we will have a much better picture of the rate of return that the portfolio needs to generate. We often find that over time, a return of 4 to 5 percent will sustain our clients' accustomed lifestyles. The investment modeling also seeks a return sufficient to keep up with inflation.

In developing investment plans, we strive to diversify them to mitigate risk. The risk that you feel emotionally able to tolerate plays a role, but the bigger question is whether your portfolio can handle that risk without wrecking your retirement plan. You may be comfortable with playing the odds, but will your portfolio be able to endure those odds if the numbers fall unfavorably? Is the risk of loss too high for the possible gain? On the flip side, do you run the risk of gaining too little to offset inflation? The best balance is to attain sufficient growth in excess of your withdrawals to maintain an increasing income for the rest of your days.

The real risk that many people face is themselves. You can complete a questionnaire and decide that you have a high tolerance for risk. But what will you do when the market takes a downturn? Will you wait until your portfolio holdings hit bottom, then panic and sell prematurely?

People do that repeatedly. They then become emotionally paralyzed and fail to reinvest. That is an aspect of human nature that can lead to investment nightmares, and it is where collaboration with a financial planner can help immensely. With a full understanding of the client's financial affairs and long-term goals, the planner can serve the crucial role of intermediary during times of potential panic.

Success comes from sticking with the plan. What are you trying to accomplish? What expenses are in your budget? Without a governing financial plan, you cannot know how to move forward. You will be guessing at whether you can meet your expenses and objectives. A successful plan requires much more than guesswork. You need assurance that you will have a lifelong income that includes the opportunity for sufficient growth to meet your goals.

BALANCING THREE ESSENTIALS

A financial plan includes both short-term and longer-term perspectives. It considers expenses that are relatively immediate as well as those that will not come for decades. We regularly review the plan to make sure that it maintains the proper balance to meet those objectives, using investments that provide objectives for preservation, liquidity, or growth.

For your needs over a three-year to five-year period, we will focus on investment vehicles that can provide you with a reasonable degree of confidence that the money will be there for you and be accessible. It needs to be safe and liquid to meet the expenses that you soon will face. As we look further out, beyond six or seven years, we seek a hedge against the inflation that surely will begin to show its effects. Allocating some growth investments becomes necessary to provide a necessary hedge.

Even if you describe yourself as risk averse, it is important to recognize that inflation remains one of the overall largest risks to your portfolio. If you do nothing to confront it, you are accepting that risk. Even at a relatively low rate, inflation can eat away at your purchasing power. The risk-averse investor who invests every cent into short-term, stable, liquid investments is actually taking on substantial risk in the long term.

Conversely, if you invest most of your money into growth and the market takes a severe downturn exactly at the same time as a major expenditure, you can seriously compromise the overall course of your retirement. For example, a major health issue could arise suddenly. An overemphasis on the growth portion of a portfolio risks invoking Murphy's Law: if something can go wrong, it will. Hindsight won't help.

The solution is a portfolio that is properly balanced among liquid, conservative, and growth investments. You can think of these as "buckets" for your money. Your liquid bucket will contain the money you will need for your cash flow for the next year or two, plus a cushion. You will have another bucket for the medium term that is allocated for moderate growth, and once it grows and matures, it can be used to refill the liquid bucket. You will have longer-term investments as well, and if those enjoy a good period of growth, the money to refill the liquid bucket can come from there, instead. That will let the medium-term bucket continue to fill.

Such a system can give your portfolio the potential to recover from market downturns. Your financial demands during that downturn will not require you to sell from your longer-term buckets. You will have safe and accessible money ready and waiting to meet your current needs.

I use the bucket analogy when explaining this system to my clients because it is a visual way to clearly explain the concept of asset allocation. I make it clear that we do not actually set up several accounts to create separate buckets. Instead, we maintain one account, and within that account, we allocate the assets among investment vehicles that function as "buckets."

For example, you would not have multiple IRAs. One IRA would be sufficient, but within it you would have a variety of investment vehicles. Some of the holdings would provide safety and liquidity for short-term spending. Other holdings within the IRA would provide growth for the medium and longer terms. Meanwhile, we try to keep at least a 3 to 5 percent cash position. This area tends to be where monies are disbursed from the portfolio for monthly living expenses. As the cash is used, we replenish it from other short-term investment vehicles.

It is important to note that different products perform differently. They are designed for specific purposes, and they should be assigned to their proper function within the portfolio. Each should be in its proper place. If money is needed quickly, you can't accept much risk. However, more risk is acceptable with assets that aren't needed for several years. Furthermore, even more risk might be acceptable with assets that won't be needed for many years or are intended for heirs following your passing.

As part of your planning, you may also decide to purchase an immediate annuity that offers an income for life. You can also choose from variable or equity-indexed annuities that include lifelong income riders. These can be expensive, so you will want a thorough cost/benefit analysis. Your financial planner can assist with thoroughly examining these products so that you can make a fully informed decision on whether to include them in your retirement strategy.

A SENSE OF COMFORT

A well-designed and balanced income plan will provide you with a sense of comfort. Ideally, retirement should not be a time of anxiety and worry. The income plan discussed previously can funnel cash directly into your checking account, similarly to when you were receiving a paycheck. That will cover your regular expenses. It is also reassuring to know that your portfolio takes into account the cost of meeting longer-term goals. Living day to day becomes easier knowing that your finances can run smoothly year by year, with regular reviews and necessary adjustments. It is imperative to have a portfolio that can weather the storms.

With this strategy, you will have created a replacement for the pension that so many people have lost. This strategy can provide you with an income that can last as long as you do, and it can also provide for your heirs. All the while, you will remain firmly in charge. After all, you are the CEO of what amounts to your family business: the wealth that you have accumulated during your working years.

CHAPTER NINE

HANDLING YOUR ESTATE

T he widow was adamant: she was not going to change the beneficiary form on her IRA, at least not yet. It was a relatively small account, less than a tenth of her total assets. Still, I had implored her several times to sign the papers. I could see that a problem was in the making.

Her concern was that if she left a share of the account to her disabled child, he no longer would qualify for medical assistance. But she didn't want to just cut him out, for fear of upsetting him.

She had two other children and did not want to appear to be playing favorites. She couldn't make up her mind about what to do. It was easier to avoid talking about it.

And so she made a de facto decision: she did nothing. One evening she had a massive stroke and didn't wake up. She had never changed the beneficiary designation to her children. The account became a headache for the child who was responsible for settling the estate, which needed to be run through probate. As a result, the estate was forced to take the distribution all in one year as a lump sum. Had she changed the designation, the assets could have been split among the children in beneficiary IRAs for each, ultimately avoiding probate.

In the end, the IRA was small enough that the tax issue was not too significant. Nevertheless, the family lost the opportunity to defer taxes for the next generation while allowing the account to continue to grow. Instead, the money came out in one lump sum. The estate had to pay income taxes on the entire IRA. This unfortunate situation could have easily been avoided.

PREPARE FOR "WHAT-IFS"

Inadequate estate planning can create significant issues for your heirs. We all have heard about deceased celebrities and others whose families squabble bitterly over money and property. Those are the extremes. You are much more likely to simply leave your loved ones a series of issues that could have been handled easily while you were living. Your inactions could unintentionally leave them burdened by many hours of tedious work as they sort through your affairs.

In the event that you die without making your intentions clear, you run the risk of igniting a feud within your own family.

Many families can handle these pressures, but many cannot. If you have neglected to carefully craft a will or trust document or failed to properly define or update beneficiaries on retirement plans and insurance policies, consider how you might ultimately be remembered. Irresponsibility breeds irritation.

A lot of people will have their documents prepared and then put them in a drawer. Fifteen years later, the papers are outdated, as their lives have changed. Don't fall into such a haphazard approach. Important documents need to be regularly monitored and updated. Typically, they include your will, trusts of various kinds, powers of attorney, and a health-care directive (living will).

If you do not bother to formulate an estate plan, you will receive one anyway. You can let the government make the decisions on behalf of you and your family, but it's unlikely that you will like how it turns out. Each state has its own process for handling estates that do not have wills or trusts in place. If you don't have at least a will, your heirs will have to get an attorney and appear in front of a judge so that an executor or personal representative can be named to handle the estate. Your heirs and family members will generally become annoyed by the protracted proceedings—not to mention the expense of hiring an attorney to sit through them.

An estate plan is imperative not only in the event of your death but also if you should become incapacitated. In either case, it is absolutely necessary for you to assign a durable power of attorney. I am not an attorney, but I have worked with attorneys often to ensure that my clients' issues, desires, and needs are addressed. If you are unable to make decisions on your own behalf, the power of attorney will allow for someone else to pay outstanding expenses and execute other important financial matters.

WILLS AND TRUSTS

Will and trust documents play the central role in the estate planning of many families. Both play key roles in the distribution of assets upon death. However, it is important to remember that a will does not avoid probate. Anything held in your personal name that you bequeath in your will must be probated.

Typically, and depending upon the size of the estate, a probate tax will be due as well. In many states, the trigger for the tax is when the estate is larger than $30,000. That being said, it takes a considerable amount of processing to accumulate the data and complete the necessary paperwork. Whether an attorney is necessary or not, there is an inherent cost. That cost includes the value of your heirs' time.

The will does not maintain any control over your assets. It just disseminates the assets. A trust, however, can provide considerable control. You can stipulate who will receive what, when they will receive it, and for what purpose. For example, if your child is the beneficiary and faces a judgment or divorce, the assets in a trust can be protected from the claims of a creditor or an ex-spouse. If you deem your child to be a spendthrift, you can set up a monthly income stream that limits access to the entire inheritance. The trust is effectively in its own estate. As such, it safeguards your legacy. You can have much of your money titled in the name of your revocable trust, which, when you pass away, becomes irrevocable.

Assets that are titled within the trust do not go through probate. Therefore, you can avoid the probate expenses and taxes, as well as the privacy issues that arise. When a will is probated, the disposition of the assets is a matter of public record, and many people would prefer to keep that information private. Retirement plans also avoid probate if the beneficiaries are alive and capable of receiving the assets. The beneficiary designation takes precedence over the will.

You want to consider your family dynamics when the question arises as to who should be appointed as trustee. If you have two children, one of whom is a good steward of money and the other is not, I would suggest that you consider hiring a professional organization to handle the trustee duty. If you appoint the good steward as the trustee, you could be unintentionally setting up the siblings for a fight. Giving power to one over the other can lead to trouble.

If you establish a trust, you must not leave it as a document sitting on a shelf. You need to fund it. You need to put assets into it, properly titled. One of the big issues with estate plans is implementation. It can cost $3,000 to $5,000, or more, to establish a complete estate plan. Of course, this depends on what you include in it. The cost of probate on a half-million-dollar estate would be about the same, but setting up a trust provides a tremendous amount of additional benefits, direction, and privacy. For larger estates, the savings are significant, including a big break just on the probate tax. It is important to note again: a revocable trust becomes irrevocable at your passing.

Irrevocable trusts come in many varieties including the charitable remainder trust, with which you can donate assets to a charity of your choice and retain control of those assets during your lifetime while receiving a regular income. A tax deduction is received for the donation, and the charity gets the balance of the trust as a lump sum, exempt from taxes, upon your passing.

Of course, that also means that children or other heirs won't be getting that inheritance. Many families use a life insurance policy to replace the wealth given to charity so that the children do not feel slighted. A death benefit also can be used to create liquid assets for your heirs upon your passing so that they are not forced to sell a property to pay the taxes due. Depending on the size of your estate, this may be appropriate. Additionally, for families leaving a business to the next generation, life insurance can serve to equalize the estate. For example, perhaps only one son is interested in continuing the business. His siblings might not want a stake in the business, but they understandably want their share of the inheritance. Life insurance solves that issue: the son gets the business, and his siblings get the life insurance payout.

INSURANCE REASSURANCE

Wealthy people who have grown their portfolios over a working lifetime may not perceive themselves as particularly well off. Outsiders, however, may have taken notice. As a result, it is important to protect yourself from liability claims that present a major risk to your estate.

It's important to know that you are properly insured on an automobile and homeowners level and that you have some umbrella liability insurance as well. Serious injuries resulting from an accident can open the estate up to significant expenses as a result of legal defense.

For example, let's say you are worth $2 million and have a home-owners insurance policy with coverage up to $300,000. One snowy morning, a teenager knocks at your door and offers to shovel your driveway. "Sure," you say and hand him $20. The kid slips and suffers severe and permanently debilitating head injuries, and his family files a lawsuit. Your insurance company sizes up the liability, decides not to take a chance or spend money on legal fees, and writes a $300,000 check to the family, washing its hands of the case.

But that's not the end of it. The family's attorney learns that you have deep pockets. The family wants more, and you end up having to hire your own legal counsel to continue the proceedings.

As you can see, your family's overall wealth could be highly vulnerable in this situation. You need to confront this possibility and talk about these issues with your financial planner and insurance professional. You need to be certain that your agent is aware of the amount of wealth at stake.

As a guideline, there should be coordinated policies for homeowners and automobile insurance along with an umbrella policy that covers at least the total net worth of the estate. Umbrella liability insurance is relatively inexpensive. A million-dollar policy for excess liability coverage might cost $500 or $600 a year, whereas a million-dollar policy to insure jewelry could cost $5,000 to $10,000 a year. The umbrella policy is worth the expense. It bridges a lot of gaps, including the cost of legal counsel, which the insurer would now be covering.

In another example, two drivers had a fender bender on a rainy evening. As the women exchanged information, they were standing between their cars. A third driver slid into one of the cars, pinning the women between them. The two resulting lawsuits claimed injuries, loss of wages, and pain and suffering. The settlement was for $5 million.

The third driver had not been cited for any wrongdoing. This was not a case of driving under the influence, driving while texting, speeding, or recklessness. This was a mishap on a slippery road. He was relatively affluent, which could have made him a target. However, he had an excess liability policy that covered up to $20 million in damage. He was well protected.

Many people are not; they might have an estate worth $1.5 million but carry only a few hundred thousand dollars in insurance. Some of the wealthiest people are also some of the most frugal by nature and may attempt to trim expenses by keeping liability coverage to a minimum. That creates a gaping hole in their coverage, and there is a lot at stake. The wealth that they hoped to pass to their loved ones could instead wind up in the hands of strangers.

This is a particularly acute concern for older drivers, whose reflexes and response times can slow down and expose them to greater liability risk. In just one moment of lapsed judgment, life savings could vanish. No matter how buoyant the market, no matter how savvy the investor, someone else could be cashing in.

A LEGACY OF MORE THAN MONEY

If you are like many people approaching or currently in their retirement years, you consider your legacy to be one of the most important elements of your planning. It is a question that looms large: What will you ultimately leave behind?

Your heirs generally will want to do the right thing, but they need guidelines as to your wishes. For example, if you want a certain piece of furniture to go to your daughter, that will usually happen if you make your intentions clear. With proper estate planning, you can provide this direction, minimize taxes and fees, and protect your privacy.

I have witnessed cases in which estates were handled improperly. Incorrect documentation can cause estate settlements to drag on for years. Meanwhile, the heirs become increasingly frustrated. It is far better to be highly specific about your wishes and to make sure that every detail is meticulously addressed. Your children may remember you as quite the stickler, but they will be smiling fondly as they reminisce.

Your planning, of course, must deal with the management of your estate and taxes and your ability to maintain control of financial affairs once you have passed on. But it also involves the memories that you will leave behind. What was your purpose here? What was it all about?

Financial planning often involves other family members—spouses, certainly, but also their grown children (to the extent that the couple wishes them to know about their financial affairs). For various reasons, parents may wish to keep some of that to themselves. However, communicating to some degree on legacy issues is simply the sign of a healthy and functional family. It is the loving husband, for example, who encourages his wife to participate in the planning even if she does not feel so inclined. Not only does she bring her own valuable perspective on family matters to the table, but he wants to protect her in the event that he dies first. (Life expectancy statistics show this as the most likely scenario.) He wants her to know and trust the advisor who will help her carry on her financial affairs as a widow.

Estate planning is primarily about money, but it is also about so much more; it is about values, ethics, and the story of who you were and what you believed. When you instill family pride and good stewardship in the next generation, your life's work is far more likely to be preserved and nurtured. In the end, that is how you pass on a true legacy.

CONCLUSION

FORWARD WITH CONFIDENCE

Not long ago, a couple came to me suggesting that they wanted to take $50,000 out of their portfolio. They didn't have a significant amount of money, but they wanted to turn their basement into an apartment for their daughter and son-in-law, who had run into severe financial difficulty. The plan was to put in a kitchen, two bedrooms, and a TV room.

I went through the math with them. I advised them that a finished basement was not likely to add much to the value of their house, so they probably would not be able to recover the cost. And I ventured to say that if they made the living arrangement too comfortable, the young couple might never move out.

"Is your objective to have them there for the rest of your lives, paying no rent, while you cover the utility bills?" I asked. Clearly it was not. They wanted the younger couple to be independent.

"How much money do you think that they would need to help get them through this gap in their life?" I asked. They figured that about $12,000 should do it. We determined together that taking an additional thousand dollars a month from their portfolio for a year or two would not reduce their probability of success by too much. They could help the kids and not sacrifice any of their own dreams. Not long after, their son-in-law got a new job, and he and their daughter were able to pay their own expenses.

Had that couple chosen to withdraw the $50,000 to redo their basement, I could not have stopped them. Still, they came to me for advice, and they sought my honest assessment. And I gave them my honest view on the matter, with facts and specifics about how the decision would influence the path of their retirement. That is what my clients hire me to do. That is how I earn their loyalty and respect.

Another couple recently came to me to talk about the distribution of their sizable estate. One of their children had been requiring considerably more help than the others. They intended to make it up to the other two children by leaving them a somewhat greater bequest.

"Do they get along?" I asked the couple. They seem surprised at my question. A lot of clients don't expect that kind of a discussion, but it is crucial to the decision. This is much more than a numbers business. This is truly a relationship business.

"Oh, they get along," the husband said. "They get along very well. I think they'd all understand why we did it this way."

I turned to his wife. "What are your thoughts?"

She looked at me and then at her husband. "I don't think that the other children would understand," she said, simply and quietly.

"Well, here's why I'm asking," I said. "This is all about your legacy. You want things to stay positive. We've all heard the stories about what can happen. Families end up divided. It's so important that they understand what you're doing and why you're doing it."

"The problem I see," the wife explained, "is that all of them seem to have such selective memories. I think there would be an issue among them unless we were there to set them straight. I've been thinking that we should break it up into three equal parts so they'll get the same." The other way could work too, she said, but only with clear and regular communication.

Her perspective was central to how we decided to proceed. I have found that to be the case repeatedly in my years of practice. Both spouses, as well as family members who will be intimately affected by the planning, must participate in the discussions. Sometimes I will see a wife deferring all of the financial matters to the husband. I need to draw her into the discussion. Women take leadership roles in many family matters, quite often including portfolio management and financial planning. And they often excel more than their husbands at understanding the family dynamics. Nurturers by nature, they see critical patterns that the husband might overlook.

You and your spouse should look upon yourselves as the co-CEOs of the family finances and think of your savings and portfolio as a family business. It is the advisor's responsibility, in the role of chief operations officer, to work within the structure of your "business" to develop, discuss, and execute a plan based on your wishes and needs. That calls for wise delegation on your part. Not just anyone will do.

Long ago, as part of a career-enrichment program, a counselor stepped me through a personality-profiling exercise. It reinforced something that I had instinctively known about myself: I have a trusting nature, and I will presume the best in people unless they prove themselves untrustworthy. That is the foundation of the two-way relationships that I have long maintained with my clients.

The counselor also told me that I was by nature an "accommodator," one who is inclined to dig deeply for solutions. It's not "accommodating" in the sense of acquiescing. It's a personality type that reaches out to others and strives to understand them.

When you are seeking a good financial advisor to help you with your retirement planning, you should find the one who best suits your personality and needs. Ask questions to find out whether he or she shares with you similar values and personality traits that can be the basis for a comfortable and productive long-term relationship.

Please do this right. You have so much to gain and so much to lose. A wise financial strategy for retirement will blend many concerns that need to be addressed, including the nuts and bolts of investment, tax, and estate management. It will also illustrate the bigger picture. You will know where the money is coming from and where it is going. You will gain a greater sense of direction and confidence as you pursue your goals and dreams. You are doing it for yourself and for the loved ones to whom you will be leaving a legacy. It can truly give you financial confidence and freedom.

I believe in boomerangs. By that, I mean that what you throw out there in life is generally what will come back to you. When you do the right thing, the right thing returns—perhaps from an unexpected direction. When you do the wrong thing, guess what? It comes back to you.

That boomerang philosophy is how I choose to run my life, and it is how I conduct my business. I strive to give everyone and everything my best shot with a steady hand, and I have seen how that can build relationships. In the end, we are in the relationship business. It all comes back to that.

ABOUT THE AUTHOR

Dan Butler began in the securities industry in 1989 and joined Raymond James Financial Services, Inc. in 1994. He is currently a member of Raymond James Financial Services Leader's Council*—recognition reserved for the top financial advisors in the firm.

Dan has gained recognition for his personalized design of individual financial plans using asset-allocation modeling, cash-flow analysis, and risk-tolerance profiles to assist high-net-worth individuals in the formulation of customized plans designed to endure multiple financial cycles. He has gained recognition for his work with corporate executives in assisting them with planning for exercising nonqualified and incentive stock options. He is recognized by the National Center for Employee Ownership as a consultant in its resource guide. Dan conducts educational seminars on long-term financial planning, retirement planning, stock options, and insurance planning.

Dan is a graduate of West Chester University. He and his family reside in West Chester, and he remains active in local church, educational, and volunteering efforts.

*2009-2016 Recipient Membership is based on prior fiscal year production. Requalification is required annually.